Inside the Nixon Administration

Inside the Nixon Administration

The Secret Diary of Arthur Burns, 1969–1974

EDITED BY
Robert H. Ferrell

University Press of Kansas

Published by the University Press of Kansas (Lawrence, Kansas 66045), which was organized by the Kansas Board of Regents and is operated and funded by Emporia State University, Fort Hays State University, Kansas State University, Pittsburg State University, the University of Kansas, and Wichita State University

Library of Congress Cataloging-in-Publication Data

Burns, Arthur F. (Arthur Frank), 1904–1987.
Inside the Nixon administration : the secret diary of Arthur Burns, 1969–1974 / edited by Robert H. Ferrell.
p. cm.
Includes index.
ISBN 978-0-7006-1730-2 (cloth : alk. paper)
1. Burns, Arthur F. (Arthur Frank), 1904–1987—Diaries. 2. United States—Politics and government—1969–1974—Sources. 3. United States—Economic conditions—1961–1971—Sources. 4. United States—Economic conditions—1971–1981—Sources. 5. United States—Economic policy—1961–1971—Sources. 6. United States—Economic policy—1971–1981—Sources. 7. Monetary policy—United States—History—20th century—Sources. 8. Nixon, Richard M. (Richard Milhous), 1913–1994—Political and social views—Sources. 9. Board of Governors of the Federal Reserve System (U.S.)—History—20th century—Sources. I. Ferrell, Robert H. II. Title.
E855.B86 2010
973.924—dc22 2010021333

British Library Cataloguing-in-Publication Data is available.

Printed in the United States of America

10 9 8 7 6 5 4 3 2

The paper used in this publication is recycled and contains 30 percent post-consumer waste. It is acid free and meets the minimum requirements of the American National Standard for Permanence of Paper for Printed Library Materials Z39.48-1992.

Contents

A photo section appears following page 82.

Introduction

Arthur F. Burns wrote this diary to hold in his mind the strengths and foibles of the leading figures of the Nixon administration, not least the president himself, and this is its attraction to present-day readers. He was a clear writer. Also a spare writer; he wasted no time in preliminaries, side issues, and irrelevancies.

The diarist could boast—though he would not have done it, he was not that sort of individual—of so many recommendations. For one thing he was near the top of the administration: he was chairman of the Federal Reserve Board. This was a time when economics held special importance, for President Nixon insisted upon closing the so-called gold window, an approximate valuation of the dollar with gold bullion. The administration removed convertibility and the dollar floated, that is, received an even more approximate value by being rendered convertible only to other currencies, whatever sort the market would allow. The consensus over many years has been that the president himself arranged this, and the diary confirms it. Such a come-to for the once almighty dollar was not Burns's idea nor that of other economists. The window closed in 1971 and the president was up for reelection the next year and wanted inflation to give advantage to the dollar for this obvious reason. Closing the gold window was connected to the expenditures of the Vietnam War and the many expensive social and other programs of the preceding Johnson administration. All this appears in Burns's diary.

As the economic problems gathered there was the more troubling one of the ineptitude of so much of Washington officialdom, and in his pointed diary entries Burns set it out, including his rapidly increasing doubt about the president himself. Burns started out in 1969 with great hope for the administration and especially the president as a national leader. His initial diary descriptions of Nixon are close to reverence: this president seemed to promise so much. One is reminded of a small but prescient campaign scene that took place in the little railroad town of

Deshler, Ohio, where Nixon met a gathering and said a few words, during which a photographer captured the remark on a sign someone held up. It read, "Bring us together." After the tumults of the Johnson administration this appeared to be such a splendid idea, and Burns thought Nixon might do it. Instead—and here is the great virtue of this diary—Burns, acutely observant, constantly talking with the president at the "W.H." or hearing the voice on the telephone, began to see a maneuvering and at times an almost insane shouting that became intensely worrisome.

Arthur Burns was a Democrat in the 1930s, a Republican in later years. He received appointments from Eisenhower, Nixon, and Reagan. He could work with Democrats and Republicans. He simply was no extremist, but sought to take the course or position that was sensible. His professional study of economics would have taught him that, if he had not inherited it from sources unknown. Above all he despaired of irrationality, which politics, he saw, easily could get into.

And behind his refusal to twist ideas rather than understand them lay his background, which was not singular for American officials but offered, if the individuals could take advantage of it, a point of view that could assist whatever were their official responsibilities. This is a rotund way of saying that Burns was not a native American. He was born in Stanislau, Austria, in 1904, the only child of Nathan Burnseig and Sarah Juran, who came to the United States when he was ten years old and settled in Bayonne, New Jersey. His father was a paint contractor. The younger Burns received a tuition scholarship to Columbia University where he took a bachelor's and master's degree in economics and supported himself as a waiter, shoe salesman, house painter, postal clerk, and summer sailor. With the degrees under his belt, he managed to become a faculty member at Rutgers University. In 1934 he obtained a doctorate in economics at Columbia and a decade later an appointment to the Columbia economics department. There he met the new president of Columbia in 1948, General Dwight D. Eisenhower, who in 1953 appointed him chairman of the Council of Economic Advisers. In Washington he met Vice President Nixon, hence the return to the capital in 1969.

But this is ahead of the point, which is that Burns's opportunities in a new country created the indelible patriotism that marked his life. He was thoroughly grateful for what this country had done for him. He knew the great danger of immodesty and advantage seeking, shunned it, could not stand it in others, noticed it sometimes almost too quickly but was seldom mistaken in appraisals for he had learned how to see it during his own remarkable life. The fact that he was a nationally known economist—an expert on business cycles, a reviser of the theories John Maynard Keynes set out in *General Theory,* a book championed by most American economists, and an opponent of the Chicago school of Milton Friedman—gave him a solid professional base for his public duties. The solidity of his self-knowledge made him impervious to the mistakes of politics. His life's journey had made him sufficiently diplomatic to abide politics and if necessary be political. But when the public interest intervened he could be counted on. What better background for the Nixon administration or any administration?

When President Carter failed to reappoint him to the Federal Reserve in 1978, Burns stayed in the capital as a member of the American Enterprise Institute until his appointment by President Reagan in 1981 as ambassador to West Germany. In 1985 he returned to the institute. In 1987 he entered Johns Hopkins Hospital for what proved a triple-bypass heart operation. He died there of complications from the surgery a few weeks later.

Two final points about the diary. First, the economic issues discussed therein, notably, the closing of the gold window.

The Nixon administration's failure to control inflation gave Arthur Burns the sure feeling that he could not trust the new president and sent his hopes on a slow descent to their low point in 1974 when the president resigned. As it happened, he could measure the actions of the officials, including the president, with whom, as chairman of the Federal Reserve Board, he found himself up against. Here he of course knew what he was up against when on the weekend of Friday through Sunday, August 13–15, 1971, together with other leading economic figures of the administration, he took a helicopter to Camp David for the national summit meeting, as he might have described the group with whom he conferred. His problem was to obtain the semblance of order as the administration went off gold, moved onto a slippery slope where the key word for inflation was "float." This was a basic change in the economic system that obtained at the Bretton Woods Conference of 1944 during the Roosevelt administration. The economic system of that earlier time necessarily had been dominated by the United States, which not only possessed most of the world's gold supply but was emerging from World War II with the world's dominant economy (aside from the Communist-dominated economy of Eastern Europe and the Soviet Union). With the Camp David accord within the U.S. government it was possible for President Nixon to announce what he described as a New Economic Policy—with more than a little resemblance, it seemed, to the Soviet plan of Lenin in the early 1920s under which the Soviets sought, not without enormous trouble and huge loss of life, to gain control of their country's economy.

The NEP sought to increase employment but was never more than a cover for just plain-vanilla inflation, which the president desired. This was apparent because of the inability of the float policy to last more than a few months. The administration had come into office bearing promises of balancing the budget, a requisite for maintaining the gold standard, and instead had produced only a new word, stagflation, meaning a stagnant economy accompanied by inflation. By 1971, with Nixon's second-term campaign getting close, something seemingly other than the usual fiscal tightening that Burns represented had to be done. But then one change had to follow another. In December it was a meeting of finance ministers at the Smithsonian that applied still another word to describe its result: a "managed" float. Fifteen months later, a suitable way to disguise the failure of management as a device, and with the president's reelection secured by the appearance of controlled change rather than the economic chaos that governed, Burns lost his confidence in the president who, at the beginning of what indeed seemed a new political era, had given every promise of abjuring politics and going over to sound principles rather than words.

The chairman of the Federal Reserve Board did not lose his

confidence with the failure of economic measures. He lost it in the political moves of the president and then, as the meaning of the White House's assistants began to sink in, the Fed chairman began to see individuals whom he considered operators rather than suitable officials carrying messages from the White House and bringing messages back to the president. This prepared the diarist for what came in the year he halted his diary, namely, Nixon's resignation.

So much for the gold window. Lastly, how the diary became available forty years later. Burns's widow—he married Helen Bernstein in 1930—gave the diary to the Gerald R. Ford Library at Ann Arbor, where it remained closed until 2008. Mrs. Burns dedicated publication rights to the people of the United States, to use the archival phrase. Hence forty years had elapsed since the diarist wrote in two spiral notebooks, one marked thirty-nine cents, the other (larger) forty-nine. Library officials in anticipation of opening the diary to readers undertook to prepare a typescript, a necessity because the diarist's handwriting was so difficult to read. They went to the length of giving the diary to Burns's secretary, Gail Veenstra, to decipher some small sections, and there are a few she could not read, duly marked in the present pages.

Whenever possible, editorial comments appear after rather than before the diary entries, and last in the comments are identifications of people. For American officials and offices the source is *United States Government Organization Manual*, published annually by the Government Printing Office.

Acknowledgments

In the Ford Library the supervisory archivist, David Horrocks, could not have been more gracious in pointing out the attractions of his holdings, especially the Burns diary; it was his enthusiasm for his material that caught my attention when the diary first opened. Without the work of Stacy Davis, who supervised Meghan Lyon and Beth Panozzo in making a transcription, I literally could not have read the diary, nor could anyone, I think. Christian Goos first brought out the original two spiral notebooks, testimonies to Burns's belief in "a penny saved." And Christian, like the other members of the staff, but I believe more so, from the outset was quick to be helpful. He anticipates what a researcher might wish and there, in a minute, it is. He is at the beginning of his career with the National Archives and will go far. Mark Fischer, formerly of the Nixon materials project, now the Ford Library, explained the taping system in the Nixon White House.

In the materials project I am indebted to Steve Green, who identified photographs that Burns displayed in his office and assisted with other photographs just at the time when the project came to an end and its staff members left for California and the newly established Nixon Library. My thanks to Nancy Mirshaw in audiovisual reference at the Ford Library for similar help in identification of photographs.

My great thanks to the Nixon biographer Melvin Small, whose book was such an assistance; it is the sort of book that sets out essentials, in suitable detail, fulfilling the very purpose of the American Presidency Series published by the University Press of Kansas. I am also indebted to Nixon biographer Irwin Gellman, whose multivolume account bases itself on a welter of unpublished and published material. The veritable cloud of prejudice about President Nixon that troubles so many historians has never concerned Gellman, who is as close to impartial as one can get.

In Bloomington, Indiana, my thanks to the research librarian Jeffrey

C. Graf, who can discover anything. My thanks go again to the word processor Betty Bradbury.

In Addis, Louisiana, across the levee from Baton Rouge, I have relied on the discernment of Beverly Jarrett, the former director of the University of Missouri Press, whose judgment about book publication is invariably correct.

At the University Press of Kansas, production editor Larisa Martin, assistant director Susan Schott, and director Fred M. Woodward all helped in every way. Fred called attention to books and at one point to a valuable Webster financial dictionary. Fred, like Beverly, knows manuscripts, also authors and editors, and pleases me every time he inquires about the health of Abby the dog.

In Ann Arbor, my thanks to the family: Carolyn, Lorin, Amanda, and Samantha.

Inside the Nixon Administration

1969 1970 1971 1972 1973 1974

In observing the inaugural of the new president of the United States—this is where Burns's diary begins—the erstwhile professor of economics at Columbia University was not quite sure what to think; he sought to use his keenest wit to measure a personality with which, if he failed, he would have to measure himself. He would not let the occasion overwhelm him; he had known Nixon's predecessor, Eisenhower, seen him inaugurated, and served in that president's first administration as chairman of the Council of Economic Advisers—therefore, he had been in the White House many times. He had known Nixon when the latter was vice president and sought to help him when Nixon ran for the presidency in 1960 and failed. At the inaugural in 1969 he hoped for the very best for the new president but one possible danger caught his observant eye.

As the first weeks of the administration passed, Burns thought the new president might be troubled by something, an inability to relax. Eisenhower was dying in Walter Reed Hospital, and Burns visited him, catching flashes of the famous smile and noticing in particular how "Ike" relaxed, took issues as they came, and did not approach them in Nixon's somewhat nervous way. However the new president had "trained himself," as Burns put it, for the work of president, he could not relax in the way his Republican predecessor had long known how to do. Almost wistfully Burns asked Eisenhower to teach Nixon how to relax.

Meanwhile, while William McChesney Martin, an old New Deal appointee, served out his term as chairman of the Federal Reserve, Burns was appointed counselor, the highest rank of presidential adviser and assigned the large task of reorganizing the sprawling cabinet departments and special offices of the executive branch.

Jan. 20 Inauguration Day was cloudy, grim. Rain or snow seemed imminent, but all that we had was a penetrating cold. What did the weather signify? That Heaven itself would not send LBJ back home with a burst of sunshine? Or that the Almighty had not yet made up his mind how to greet RN? However that may be, the President-to-be had no doubts when he appeared at the top of the stairs to the Capitol. I had never seen eyes sparkle so. He stood erect, with chest protruding a bit. There was a look of exaltation about him. What was he thinking then? Not of the awesome responsibility he was about to assume. What then? I felt that in that solitary moment he had relived his whole life, that he saw the boy grow to manhood, and the man—wanting fiercely to be president—was about to become that, just as he had dreamed and planned. It was not a moment of humility, dedication, or prayer but rather a moment of triumph and fulfillment. And so it might well be, for Presidents too are human. Yet, I would have felt better if his head were bowed and his body trembled some.

Jan. 21 My appointment with the President was set for 4 p.m. I gave him my report on prospective legislation and executive action. I had worked most intensely for a period of 5 weeks preparing the document. I felt it was a good report, certainly a useful one, and that it would help the President measurably over his first four months. The Pres. glanced over it, then proceeded to describe my new job. I just gasped. I had expressed disinclination previously to a W.H. post. I still felt that way, and I wanted to protest—to plead a misunderstanding. But the Pres. did not give me a chance to plead or explain. He just smiled, waved aside my inarticulate but perfectly clear reluctance to take the post, told me what he wanted me to do at the Cabinet meeting next day, then started walking out of his room. I caught him at the door, asked whether he had heard of Martin's reluctance to leave around January 1. He answered that he knew, but that he was not concerned, for Martin would get out as he had previously arranged with him, that—after all—he had handled tougher problems than this in his life. He then took me to the Cabinet Room & showed me my seat.

Jan. 22 I gave my report. There was a good deal of discussion. The Pres. was in fine style. I watched his every word and gesture closely. Here, very plainly, was a man who knew how a President should act. And how could it be otherwise? He had, after all, trained himself for many years for his new job. I could not help but feel that, with average luck, he will make a very good President.

Feb. 3 Recent days have been long and hard. I've attended too many meetings. And I have seen the President nearly every day. His style continues to be impressive. He clearly likes his job. He *wants* to be a good President, really a president of *all* the people. I can hardly recall a single partisan utterance. This does not surprise me, but would the world believe it. His days are long, but that is general around here. He drives the people around him—Cabinet, staff, etc. That is as it should be. I handed him the rest of the directives I had prepared on the basis of my report. He liked the report, and insisted I move rapidly on every part of it, which I have now done.

Day began with a long meeting of Urban Affairs Council. Moynihan was the star of the occasion. We planned a meeting for next Saturday when the draft of a message on OEO would be unveiled. I helped to speed this. After meeting, I saw the President & he reviewed rest of directives. I told him of the Executive Order I had prepared on strict schedule reporting. He liked the idea, despite Bryce's concern that we might benefit from occasional delay or haste in reporting. He looked tired, called in Mayo, and told him that he ruled against him on the advance payment for food grains. He did not find this easy. When Mayo left, he talked about the NSF & his inclination to rule against Mayo again. I told him I thought I could straighten this out without any intervention on his part. This I later did. Mayo agreed to give NSF 10 million, & Du Bridge accepted, though he wanted 15. Awfully busy after that. Called Treasury & prodded them on several messages I wanted this week. Met later with Garment to discuss organization of voluntary efforts. Discussed message—electoral with Phillips of Justice Dept. & [Barren?]. Outlined what I thought message should cover. Earlier at lunch, I suggested to Bryce that we must organize ourselves for the purpose of reducing the number of conflicts that go to R.N. Perhaps a committee with Haldeman, Ehrlichman, Bryce & myself. Bryce thought plan was good.

[The OEO, Office of Economic Opportunity, was the administrative office for the Johnson administration's antipoverty programs. It became a target for breakup by the Nixon administration, which sought to abandon OEO programs or shift them to other offices. The OEO, it turned out, possessed more staying power than Republican reformers, including plain reformers such as Burns, anticipated.

Daniel Patrick Moynihan was assistant to the president for urban affairs, Bryce N. Harlow was assistant to the president for legislative affairs, Robert P. Mayo was director of the Bureau of the Budget (BOB), and Leonard Garment was special consultant to the president. The reference to NSF is to the National Science Foundation. In addition, this entry contains the first mention of the president's two top White House assistants whom he brought from California. H. R. Haldeman's title was Assistant to the President; he served as chief of staff. John D. Ehrlichman appears in the *United States Government Organization Manual: 1969–70* (Washington, D.C.: Government Printing Office, 1969) as counsel to the president.]

Feb. 6 Days are so long that I have no chance to write even a few notes. Had meeting with President today. Gave him a few additional directives. He waxed eloquent about their usefulness, about my contributions, and industry. He liked particularly the directive to the [s?] agencies because they meant that ours will be an open administration. Then pitched into the waste of government—the multiplication of staffs, and the tendency of his own appointees to behave like the old crowd. His understanding of Parkinson's Law is complete. He wanted me to draw up a sharp directive on need to reduce size of staff. Don't quite know why he asked me to do this, since this is a BOB responsibility. Later I took this up delicately with Mayo—a genial, competent, but not very effective man. Sec'y Kennedy came to see about a problem he had with Kissinger. Latter wants Nat. Sec. Coun. to handle international monetary policy, and has already made staff appointments in [Intel sem.?] area. Kennedy is rightly indignant about all this, but he showed some tendency to compromise, I counseled that he stand firm and he agreed to do this. Earlier in day met with Kennedy and others on problem of distributing direct controls on foreign lending and investing. Stans and McCracken urged caution to the point of timidity. Kennedy and I were for bolder action. Martin, as usual, supported both groups.

[In the early days of the administration the wily Henry A. Kissinger, assistant to the president for national security affairs, his training being entirely in academic matters from his tenure in the lower reaches of the administration of Harvard University, was already poaching on the reservation of Secretary of the Treasury David M. Kennedy. It is, incidentally, an interesting question whether Kissinger was able to do this because, as most of the writers on President Nixon assert, the president was much more concerned about international affairs than domestic issues and had decided to take over the former from whatever cabinet department possessed them, or whether Kissinger himself advanced this project. Maurice H. Stans was secretary of commerce and Paul W. McCracken was chairman of the Council of Economic Advisers.]

Feb. 7 Met with Kissinger and Kennedy, Kissinger proved agreeable, so that the jurisdiction issue will be solved, probably, without bringing issue to President. Later at Cabinet meeting, Mitchell—efficient, blunt, cynical, self-confident, imperfectly informed—agreed against electoral message. President wavered, then acquiesced, asking Mitchell and me to prepare a letter in which he would urge Congress to act but not tell Congress how or on what to act. Clearly, RN has lost interest in problem, and Mitchell won—at least temporarily—a debate that he should have lost. For the decision means that President is avoiding leadership, that he is also going against his campaign pronouncement, even against his own announcement to leaders, a few days back, to send a message (not letter) in about a week. I must find a way of protecting President against the consequences of a very hasty judgment. I do not think I can convince Mitchell—he wants to duck issue; but the President should reexamine his decision and I'll try to win him over on the compelling moral grounds if I can. Today, for first time, President was thinking in partisan terms, but I really feel that he wasn't thinking at all. He has too many other things on his mind.

[John N. Mitchell was attorney general.]

Feb. 10 The Vice President has lately been involving himself in all sorts of duties. RN recently remarked that the VP was too busy building up a staff. What V-P wanted me to know was that, since I would be lunching with Romney, he did not favor a Cabinet Committee on Voluntary Action because Finch and Shultz were opposed to it, that in such a committee Romney would be chairman, so that others would appear to be working for Romney, thus it therefore was best not to have a committee, but let Romney spearhead the effort. I agreed to get Romney to do this. He acquiesced readily, expressed suspicion over Finch's ambition, talked freely about campaign; said flatly that Rockefeller had used him and that he never promised or gave Rockefeller any support, but he mistrusted Rocky because he was a spender. Later he called me, as did Agnew, to say that Finch and Shultz really did not object to Committee. Curious how grown men can waste time. When I checked with Finch, he explained he was for Committee provided it was temporary. Also told me I should know that Mrs. Nixon had strong distaste for Mrs. Romney. I still wonder why I should know this.

After leaving Romney, went to meeting on personnel problems. Young Fleming explained purpose: to make more jobs available for Republicans. A very ineffective though likeable young man.

[George W. Romney was secretary of housing and urban development; Robert H. Finch secretary of health, education, and welfare; George P. Shultz secretary of labor. A stalwart of the administration, Shultz in 1970 became director of the Office of Management and Budget, which was the former Bureau of the Budget. He thence became secretary of the treasury. The president proposed an all-volunteer army, a change from the Selective Service Act, because of unpopularity of the draft for the Vietnam War. After appointing a commission he announced the end of the draft during his campaign for reelection in 1972, to take effect the next year.]

Feb. 11 Sent RN a letter urging a crash rescue on welfare problem. Also a memorandum suggested electoral reform message. RN's treatment of this at preceding campaign meeting suggested either indifference to electoral reform or spinelessness; probably latter. With John Mitchell, it's something else—he's a tough-minded, cool cynic. I hope to rekindle RN's idealism.

Went over Executive Order on curbing gov. employment that Mayo drew up. What a weak & ineffective pronouncement!

Feb. 12 Gov. Rockefeller spoke at meeting of Urban Affairs Council. The crisis in state & local finance was his theme. The remedy, of course, was more money from Fed. Gov't for welfare & education. The surtax he would make permanent, therefore. A characteristic performance by a super-spender. Later a discussion of Minority Enterprise program by Commerce Dept. Curious & interesting to see Stans trying to find something to do. The fact that this over acting (with sizable staff) promises to [?] the Foundation for Voluntary Action doesn't trouble him at all. Next a review of Moynihan's message on OEO—an eviscerated, long-winded document. My argument against issuing it goes unheeded. Fortunately, at afternoon meeting, RN insists that it either be beefed up or dropped. Former is decided; and it is an understandably correct decision.

As I watch our Cabinet in action, I wonder more & more whether or how they differ from the LBJ people. They push for their departments, care not about money, rely on LBJ's people, and talk like them. If this continues, people over the country will be asking what promises for change we are fulfilling. Fascinating to watch cabinet officers becoming so quickly the prisoners of the career civil servants.

[Earlier Burns mentioned Daniel Patrick Moynihan and the Urban Affairs Council. During the campaign Nixon had spoken of the waste, inefficiency, and even foolishness of much of the social legislation of the Johnson administration. Many Americans, he knew, felt that way about Model Cities, the Job Corps, Head Start, and aid to higher education (if it were not their own children). The Republicans victorious, the question was what to do. The president was charmed by Moynihan, a Harvard sociologist, Democrat, and fascinating talker. Burns too liked to hear Moynihan talk but anticipated budget trouble and foreign exchange trouble and beheld Moynihan and other "spenders" overwhelming the administration. After much conversation nothing happened to reform or eliminate the Johnson social programs. Moynihan left the Nixon administration in 1970.]

Feb. 13 Meeting of Committee on Economic Policy today. President in relaxed form. Paul McCracken presented the statement he plans to make for Joint Ec. Committee. Not a very good statement, at least from viewpoint of President. RN caught some of the flaws; my own critical comments were restrained. George Shultz contributed sensibly. The statement itself could have been Ackley's or Okun's. Hardly a criticism of LBJ regime.

Lunch with Al Gruenther. Caught up on Eisenhower. Wonderful report about his state of mind. Too bad the touch of ileitis last Friday caused postponement of my meeting with DDE. Gruenther promised to check on Tom Gates' view of all-volunteer armed force.

Saw Bob Haldeman. He's concerned about [?] of staff. He continues to puzzle me. He's no Sherman Adams—that's sure. Loyal, efficient within limits—yes; but not a driver nor outstanding organizer. Relaxed dinner at President's in honor of Brosio, Laird commented on Hampton man as possible Vice-Chairman of Commission for All-Volunteer Armed Force. Opposed to Hershey serving. Talked of discontinuation of practice of White House staff putting [?] on DOD staff unless Haldeman approves. Apparently others have been doing so. A curious lack of order.

Romney called to say he approved my concept of coordination, which involved reduction of duplication even if HUD or some other dep't has to give up some function now allotted to it by law.

Flood of mail, fortunately, is beginning to slacken.

Called P. McCracken about taking a look at his revised statement. This unavoidable since President wanted to see it. Paul seemed disturbed. Too bad that he worries so much about his status.

[Alfred M. Gruenther had retired from the army and was a longtime bridge partner of Eisenhower. Sherman Adams was chief of staff in the Eisenhower administration. Manlio Brosio, the retired secretary general of the North Atlantic Treaty Organization, received the Medal of Freedom. Thomas Gates was former secretary of defense, Melvin R. Laird current secretary. Lewis B. Hershey was adviser to the president on manpower mobilization and the army's longtime head of the draft.]

Feb. 14 Saw President, gave him several directives. He approved radical plan on welfare, but expressed skepticism about results. I told him I'd like to have Scranton with me. He approved despite doubt expressed by Haldeman and Harlow, who feared the VP might feel hurt. President angrily said that what Scranton would do would not conflict with VP. Beyond that, he didn't really care; we had some jokes about the VP and that was that.

President wanted me to talk to Garment and test out his suitability for head of OEO. I did this at lunch, Garment is brilliant, but his skill as an administrator is doubtful.

Cole brought in new head of SBA—a Mexican, described by others as weak, but an appointment that was promised by Tower. He looked mighty weak indeed.

[William W. Scranton was former governor of Pennsylvania. Kenneth R. Cole, Jr., was special assistant to the president. SBA was the Small Business Administration, and John G. Tower was a Republican senator from Texas.]

Feb. 15 Had lunch with Finch and he seemed to approve of my research project on welfare. He expressed grave concern about model cities program—its terrific cost which would mount and its threat to federal system. Moynihan, who came over, seemed—much to my surprise—to agree.

Later saw President who agreed to take my advice on electoral reform message. I was much pleased by this change in his view.

My first visit with Eisenhower. He looked frail at first; but soon he had his golden smile and everything was as before. He commented that there are times when he wants to let go, that he had enough; but he did not linger on this. Soon became animated. Talked about a book he was starting, which would focus on the role of the individual in society—his responsibility, his concern for others as the way to solve our social ills. He asked many questions. I suggested he teach RN how to relax.

Eisenhower, at beginning of a meeting, particularly with someone he liked and trusted, would talk about his problems, about the meeting he just had, often swearing and yelling all over the place, and this worked out the poison in him. Only then was he ready to turn to problems of his caller. RN does not do this; he turns at once to business at hand. But his mind, quite clearly, is often still on the meeting he had just concluded. Eisenhower's technique of relaxation, also his habit of having a social visit now & then during the working day, would do RN much good—provided, of course, he could do it. The advice would probably be fruitless; every man must learn his own way; but I thought DDE might coach RN. DDE promised to do so.

Feb. 17 Urban Affairs Council met with President in the chair and John Gardner performing, as head of Urban Coalition. His talk was unimpressive. Before meeting, had breakfast with Max Fischer—an extremely well-intentioned industrialist and philanthropist. Fischer has strong faith in voluntary programs for cities. After Urban Affairs Council meeting Fischer commented that he then met Gardner for first time. Worked some more on Electoral College message, and got into good shape.

Feb. 18 Nothing very important emerged at the Legislative Leaders meeting. First, Blount's report on the new system of appointing postmasters. Hardly much enthusiasm for this dramatic shift of merit system; but they went along. Next, report on OEO message. Leaders seemed to sense that all we may be doing is to shift activities around—from OEO to HEW & Labor. They pointed out that real objective was to achieve financial economy or better administration or both. This most badly needed. Later I drafted memorandum for President to send to all members of cabinet, stressing this obvious point and also the need to stop talking about coordination of activities, if all this means is coordination of duplication. The need, of course, is to stop the duplication. Finally, I recited briefly the new messages that will be ready this week.

Saw John Gardner but couldn't tell what he sought. A good but indecisive man.

Saw RN late in afternoon, with Bryce & Ehrlichman. Turned out to be a very political meeting, but I got several directives out of the way; also got approval of the Commission on an All-Volunteer Army. President is getting rid of Bliss, and replacing him with Morton & Chotiner on the Republican National Committee. President got talking about his trip abroad, and Sargent Shriver's name came up, indicated something I did not know, I had thought that Shriver turned down UN post. But RN explained he wouldn't take him in the end, since Shriver had laid down an unacceptable condition—namely, that he must also take a hand in domestic policy. What a damned fool that lacquered fellow is! More stupid than I had realized.

President showed concern, as well he might, about the failure of Cabinet officers to get several reliable aides to turn to in their departments. He's troubled about Finch's appointment of a crew of liberals to his staff; asked me to talk to Finch about this. RN is also concerned about the VP, who—undoubtedly innocently—took an independent stand at legislative leaders meeting. Agnew means well, but he lacks the instinct to realize that VP can function only through tolerance of the President; that he must not assume an independent position when Congressional leaders are around; that he must either be silent, or echo the P's voice, or reinforce the Pres' position. Poor Bryce will have to tell poor Agnew. But will poor Agnew learn?

[Winton M. Blount was postmaster general; the post office lost its cabinet status in 1971 when it became the postal service. Ray C. Bliss of Ohio was chairman of the Republican National Committee. Rogers C. B. Morton was secretary of the interior and Murray M. Chotiner was general counsel, Office of the Special Representative for Trade Negotiations. Sargent Shriver was a brother-in-law of President Kennedy.]

Feb. 19 Met with Hinder and Ikard of American Petroleum Institute. They want a Cabinet Committee to reexamine oil import quotas. I wish such things didn't come my way. Went to a briefing of the President by State Dept fellows on trade problems with Europe. I kept wondering whom the State Dept fellows represented. They didn't even talk to the President about the new border taxes of Common Market. And they greatly exaggerated what textile quotas would do to Europeans. This, after all, is mainly an Asiatic problem. I could not help but intervene & clarify matters for RN. That was why I went to briefing in first place. President appreciated this; he called me later in evening to thank for the clarification & ask for a statement on European protectionism. He also complained about newspaper reaction to OEO message. Not clear to me whether he thought the reporting was unfair or the actions taken by us were much too mild; so that people think that we're accepting the anti-poverty program as is and merely moving some pieces around. Wanted to see about this tomorrow morning.

Learned during day that Ash is back in the picture, trying once more to build an empire for himself. At least I succeeded in making sure that McGeorge Bundy doesn't get on the committee.

[Frank N. Ikard was president of the National Petroleum Institute. Roy L. Ash was director of the Bureau of the Budget. McGeorge Bundy was national security adviser in the Kennedy and Johnson administrations.]

Feb. 20 President remained in an angry mood. Wanted me to draft directive to Shultz to the effect that Job Corps was a failure and that it will be phased out, also a directive to Finch that Head Start was inexcusably inefficient, and that he wanted a housecleaning, not a new housekeeper. Moynihan later raised objections, protested that any such published pronouncement would be a "disaster." At first, President made the language of my directive stronger. But he agreed to postpone any public pronouncement provided Shultz, Finch, Moynihan, and I come up with a hard program of reform by March 12 or 13 (I don't recall).

Later in day attended a briefing of President on international monetary problems. Volcker troubled me, gave a stupid reply to President's question why the British are interested in raising price of gold, and I had to clarify the matter. Volcker sounded like another Fowler or Barr.

[Paul A. Volcker, who followed Burns as chairman of the Federal Reserve Board, was undersecretary of the treasury for monetary affairs. Henry H. Fowler was secretary of the treasury in the Johnson administration, and Joseph W. Barr was undersecretary.]

Feb. 21 Several of us met with Haldeman and discussed failures of coordination. I commented on my meeting with Hinder and Ikard, who proposed a Cabinet review of oil import quotas; and that, as I later learned, President asked Ellsworth at about same time (possibly earlier) to take oil administration out of Interior and put it in White House. As a way of dealing with this sort of problem, Bryce and I proposed frequent meetings (1) to compare our observations, (2) call problem & one another's attention, (3) plan "visible" activities a few days or two ahead. I agreed to act as chairman. We agreed to meet at 6 that day, & to meet daily for a brief experimental period.

[Robert Ellsworth was a presidential assistant.]

Feb. 22 Chaired long meeting at Treasury to discuss one-bank holding company bill. Charles Walker defended his bill ably but he's too involved emotionally. Later in day met with Ellsworth, who outlined the oil problem and sought my aid. His suggestion that oil administration be handled by my office was unacceptable to me. Ellsworth struck me as able, sensible, but indecisive.

[The proposed one-bank holding company bill contained a loophole by which a holding company that owned only one bank could engage in all sorts of other types of business, such as selling insurance, underwriting securities, and the like, evading restrictions on such operations by banks. In fact a measure passed that did limit such diversification through one-bank holding companies. Charles E. Walker was undersecretary of the treasury.]

Feb. 23 Saw Pres. off from Andrews Air Force Base, on his trip to Europe. Rained hard.

Feb. 24 Governor Scranton came and we discussed (1) his working on grant-in-aid programs for my shop, as he had agreed to do earlier, (2) his assuming charge of OEO. President had expressed interest in his doing that; and Scranton showed interest. He wanted to know what General Accounting Office would recommend about OEO, whether it, in particular, would recommend its discontinuance. This of interest to me and I promised to see Staats, also to inform President (abroad) of Scranton's interest in OEO job, and to set up appointment for him with the President.

[Elmer B. Staats was comptroller general, hence head of the GAO.]

Feb. 25 Had breakfast with Ellsworth & Senator Cotton to discuss the interest of New England in a new oil refinery at Matthisport. Agreed to arrange a meeting with Pres. at which time the N. Engl. Republican Senators can tell Pres. this problem.

Lunched with Bill Martin, who talked loosely about finance, as always, then apologized to me for his comment about my shortcomings for Fed. position. I shrugged it off as a triviality. But I'll never understand his conduct. Poor fellow, he thinks he owns the Fed and has suddenly discovered that he is so indispensable that job must not go (though law requires it) to anyone else. Pathetic slob!

Talked to Wallis and Meckling about Commission on All Volunteer Army. Hope to get Meckling as Reserve Director.

[Norris Cotton was a senator from New Hampshire. W. Allen Wallis was president of the University of Rochester and a noted economist. William H. Meckling was a faculty member.]

Feb. 26 Saw Stans, who indicated that GAO study shows that Job Corps has had no measurable effect on employment or income, that Head Start has been run inefficiently, that OEO should continue for a while anyhow.

Feb. 27 Ran over a half dozen subjects with Sec'y Kennedy. He continues to impress me favorably. He agreed that expenditures cuts were desirable & that we might then be able to cut surcharge in half.

Discussed Commission on All-Volunteer Army with Tom Gates, who agreed to take post as chairman. Tom is skeptical of idea but I think he will make good chairman. Some of his suggestions for members on the commission were good.

Bryce and I discussed our differences about presidential messages; Bryce feels they should be very few & very selective; for if there are many, interest will diminish, & President will be frequently defeated. I agreed, except for next 2 months when it is important to convey to the country the image of dynamic leadership. Bryce seemed to give way.

President had told Bryce previously that he would not send up message on one-bank holding companies. I argued that President should reconsider, for this is the most important economic legislation, I thought, we had this year. If such holding companies are not regulated, entire economic system may change in 10 or 20 years, with 50 or 60 industrial financial complexes controlling the country. Bryce was impressed; he had thought this was just a piece of technical legislation.

Feb. 28 Met with Shultz, Kennedy, Moynihan to discuss President's ideas about Job Corps and Head Start. Moynihan seems to think that whatever displeases liberals is a disaster. He is blind to the importance of the President's retaining of his political power base.

March 2 Went to airport to greet Pres. on arrival. He looked focused & confident. Said to me "I saw a lot of your banker friends abroad."

March 4 Talked with Romney about life insurance plan of promoting building in ghetto areas. Straightened out some things with Haldeman. I did not like learning from Bryce, who heard from Flanigan, who heard from Haldeman that President did not want Scranton for OEO. This made no sense to me, and I told H. as much. I can take failure and frustration; but I cannot take sheer confusion. H. does not seem very bright; but he saw my point. Finally, he arranged appointment for Scranton. Later I went over more of the confusion with Haldeman and we agreed—early morning meetings to keep informed of President's plans so that we can serve him properly. Whether the new plan will work or not, time alone will tell. The Six O'clock Club has surely not been a howling success and I have cut it back to 2 meetings a week.

[Peter M. Flanigan was assistant to the president.]

March 3 Learned at said gathering from Bryce that President did not want Scranton for OEO; that he wanted Walter Thayer; and that this information came from Flanigan. This sounded most extraordinary & unbelievable. Had not the President changed his mind, as he clearly had every right to do, why did I have to learn this by accident?

[Walter N. Thayer was a Republican lawyer in New York City.]

March 4 Saw Romney about plans of Life Insurance group to enlarge its activity in ghettoes. Romney was more interested in housing loans than business loans. Curious, since he professes to believe in expansion of minority enterprise. Apparently, the prosperity of HUD is the stronger passion.

Flanigan confirmed Bryce's story about Scranton, and he got this story from Haldeman. A check with Haldeman brought further confirmation. But I protested procedure, and Haldeman agreed to a meeting of Scranton with President. It appears that Haldeman's got things confused, as he has frequently done before.

March 5 Had lunch with a group of Conservative journalists. I argued that country was badly divided before the election, that Nixon's major first task was to heal the wounds and unify the country; that this accounted for the appointment of Democrats, the retention of OEO, the failure to cut the budget; that Nixon was not ready to move in a more conservative direction; that he would insist that the Job Corps is phased out; that he would launch a massive voluntary program for improving urban life; that he would propose tax credits for banking investment in poverty areas and for job training; and that I saw some hope of cutting expenditures for fiscal 1970 by 3 billion dollars and cutting surcharge in half. This impressed the journalists; but the past is clear and the future is still a haze.

Meeting with President and Scranton surprised me. RN has a uniquely effective Presidential style; but he is not very effective when he invites someone to do a job. A President can tell a man that he is God's own answer to a prayer. RN doesn't proceed this way (Finch tells me that this is a chronic deficiency; that RN has never been able to ask someone to do something for him or to contribute money). RN did nothing of the sort. I had to intervene to explain that RN was asking Scranton to take the OEO job. After that, President went overboard, told Scranton that he was not satisfied with Moynihan in the sphere of devising urban programs, that he wanted Scranton not only to take OEO but to take charge of urban programs as a whole. This looseness of assignment has caused trouble before, and I wondered how much more it would cause before RN became more precise. I later explained to Scranton what RN really had in mind (or should have had in mind).

March 6 Council on Urban Affairs meeting was devoted to summer program for youngsters—a very expensive governmental program of questionable utility. RN was at his best. He saw through the rhetoric, was willing to go along (a blackmail program), but would not accept the lyrical message that had been drafted.

Had a long meeting with President. I warned him about the War on Hunger that Hardin was starting; that such political talk may create a problem where none really exists. We agreed that facts must be established, that talk will be suspended until then, that if hunger (insufficient caloric intake, something quite different from malnutrition) prevails we would move to wipe it out, but that we didn't believe it existed and that we must discourage loose talk (Martin later showed me that RN may have started the war against hunger by talking loosely and dramatically about this when he addressed D of Ag. Employees).

I also urged that we drop the fatalism into which we had fallen concerning fiscal policy; that expenditures can and should be cut and that surcharge can be then cut in half; RN liked idea and asked me to get the thinking of Mayo, Paul and Kennedy. I explained that I already had except for Paul.

We talked about urban program. This time RN asked me to do what he yesterday asked Scranton. Fortunately, I do not take him literally, but I respect the sentiment that underlies the expression. RN is worried about the urban program. In this he is justified, and I must take a more active role.

President asked me to come back next morning.

[Clifford M. Hardin was secretary of agriculture; "Paul" is Paul McCracken.]

March 7 Had breakfast with some 20 journalists—Sparling's group.

Saw President. I brought him around on the one-bank holding company act; he had not understood it before and took Bryce's view that he should shun it without examining question on the merits.

[Well before Burns became chairman of the Federal Reserve Board he saw the administration heading into a crisis over balancing the budget, which in turn would bring, eventually, a crisis over the gold window—over the highly political business of abetting the inflation part of stagflation that the administration publicly had pledged to stop. This, in turn, took him into the issue of a guaranteed annual income for the poor, advocated by Moynihan, which the president preferred to describe as a negative income tax. James M. Sparling, Jr., was assistant to the president for legislative affairs.]

Aug. 18 Several months have passed since I've made my entries in this diary. They have been busy months—16 hour days commonly, 7 days a week. I've just lacked the time or energy to write out my thoughts. But I now have a bit of leisure, with the President away in San Clemente, and I must record a few events or impressions while my memory is still fresh.

One activity that has occupied much of my time in recent months is welfare reform. At a meeting in Key Biscayne, my first there, I detected that the President was leaning toward the so-called family security system—essentially, a guaranteed income of the negative income tax variety. This disturbed me greatly, and I set about developing an alternative plan for welfare reform. I wrote numerous memoranda on this; but my discussions of this with the President were few, brief, and inconsequential.

I dissuaded, however, the President of one thing—that a work requirement must be embodied in this plan for welfare reform. He announced this at a meeting of the Urban Affairs Council, repeated this on various occasions, and the point even got across to Finch, Moynihan, and others.

But while the President agreed to this much, he finally decided to include the "working poor" in his plan for welfare reform. This had no place in my scheme; this would mean adding 13 million to the welfare rolls.

The President struggled with his decision when he left on his trip around the world. From California, he sent word to Ehrlichman to proceed with the family security plan, stressing however the work requirement also. In Bucharest he had renewed doubts, and considered omitting the working poor. But before he got back, he had made up his mind firmly to proceed with the family security idea and bring the working poor under the welfare umbrella.

The President returned from his world tour on a Sunday. Next day, on Monday, Ehrlichman called, he had to see me promptly, and he came to the office. "I have been asked by the President to inform you," he said, "that you should not worry about the family security plan. The President has decided to come out for it; but he wants you to know that he does not think the plan will get anywhere, and that you therefore should not worry." I found this pronouncement astounding. First, is the President playing a purely political game? Second, if that is the case, why doesn't he tell me this directly? Why does he send an emissary? Does he lack the courage to face me? All these thoughts ran through my mind, and central to these thoughts was my concern for the future of the country. Once again, I found myself asking the question: Have I misjudged

Nixon? Does he have real convictions? I thought that was so when I first entered the Administration; otherwise, an appointment in the White House would have made no sense to me. But my doubts on this score had been multiplying in recent weeks and months.

The Cabinet meeting at Camp David was further revealing. The evening before, the President assiduously avoided me. I did not mind, the embarrassment was his, not mine. At the Cabinet meeting proper, he showed special deference to me. The family-security plan was discussed. I asked numerous questions, disguised to bring out the weaknesses of the plan. I made my critical comments softly; there was no need to press; everyone knew where I stood and why, especially the President. The debate was inconsequential, except for Agnew's blunt and courageous remarks. Others, who opposed the plan, knowing the President had made his decision, spoke meekly in criticism, when they spoke at all. At the end, the President announced his decision; and after luncheon, he announced he hoped for full support from all.

The next day the President came to the staff meeting. He seemed bent on confronting me, in particular. He went out of his way to praise my labors—the task forces, the directives, and so on. He called on the staff to support the [?], his domestic package—meaning particularly the welfare reform. He asked the staff to go on TV (which could only mean Moynihan and me, the former needing no persuasion) and talk and talk more to members of the press, the governors, Congressmen, etc.

That reference to support on TV was especially significant, since Klein had already asked me a day or two earlier to appear on ABC. I gave him no decision at the time.

The problem before me was painfully difficult. Do I resign? Nothing would have pleased me more, except for the fact that my resignation would have proved a political bombshell. To leave quietly is one thing, but in the circumstances that was out of the question; and I was not prepared, in view of an old friendship, to do damage to the President. But do I stay on and do nothing to support the President? This would be almost as bad. Whether or not the rest of the world noticed, my position in the W.H. would have become impossible. Everyone would have said

"Unless Arthur has his way, he will sulk and sabotage." At best, I would henceforth be ignored, at worst I would be treated with utter damnation and contempt.

Since I was not ready to embarrass the President by resigning forthwith, I decided to give him—for a decent interval anyhow—such support as I morally could. I agreed to go on TV; and this proved easy for me, since I could justly emphasize the work legislation, the work incentive, the work requirement, etc. Fortunately, I did not have to discuss the federalization of the welfare program—which the W.H. propagandists described as some kind of decentralization; nor did I need to discuss the working poor. Neither Senator Mondale nor the nonprofit men knew enough to ask the tough questions, which was what I expected.

Having done my duty and having spoken the truth (though not the entire truth) on TV, I rode back in the car and comforted myself with the thought that I had done my hard duty without violence to the truth, and that the ordeal was at last over. The driver informed me that the White House operator had radioed that I phone in promptly, I somehow knew that it was the President calling.

So it was. He talked for about 15 minutes, waxed lyrical about my TV remarks, thanked me for supporting him, explained how much my loyalty meant to him, thanked me for insisting on the work requirement, thanked me for saving him from the trap of a guaranteed income, etc. The President was clearly in a euphoric mood; he wanted me to rejoice with him; he wanted me to know that he appreciated my advice though he did not take it as far as the working poor were concerned. I merely told him that the speech came over beautifully on TV, and that I appreciated his thoughtfulness in calling me.

A half hour later, he called again. This time the conversation lasted 3 minutes rather than the earlier 15. I understood the first call, but was puzzled by the second. Did the President remember that he had just called?

Had he been drinking? Or was he so carried away, in such an exalted mood, that he had to shriek his joy and keep embracing and re-embracing everyone he thought of? The President just kept repeating how much my loyalty meant to him, that he knew I had to swallow a bitter pill, that I had saved him from the guaranteed income scare, that I helped him recapture what he always believed, that the new welfare plan—whether sound or not—was at least exciting, that it showed daring and initiative. I did not disagree; I could not hurt him in his hour of triumph.

Not any of this was any surprise to me. With the success of Apollo II just behind him, with the cheering of multitudes in 8 or 9 countries still music in his ears, the President—who had previously shown an [?] to be considered bold and daring, particularly by the liberals and intellectuals—was bound to throw caution to the winds, and embark on an adventure reminiscent of the social dreaming and histrionics of FDR.

Unhappily, once the plan is better understood—particularly the sterility of the work incentive—the President will be attacked by both the right and the left; and he will not be able to comfort himself with the thought that he must therefore be doing what is really the best. That is my single prediction; the rest is spelled out in my numerous memoranda on this mad adventure.

[Herbert G. Klein was director of communications for the executive branch. Walter F. Mondale was a senator from Minnesota. Apollo II was the moon landing.]

Aug. 21 The Washington press is almost pathologically concerned about who in the Executive scheme of things is "winning" and who is "losing." I couldn't care less about any of this personally. I've had my share of so-called successes—getting the budget trimmed twice, revenue sharing, mass transit financing, [?] authority, the work requirement in welfare reform, plus all the directives and their fruit, some quite "bad." But I've had my "failures" and—as I take stock on my farm in Vermont—I take a certain pride (I hope not perversely) in the "failures," perhaps more than the "successes." There is, after all, a lasting quality about truth, and these failures were achieved in the course of fighting for it.

There was the fight against hunger. Nixon made some comments about eliminating hunger in Dept. of Ag. speech. Hardin began talking about 5 million people going hungry. Where's the evidence? I kept urging. Then the tune changed; it wasn't so much hunger as it was malnutrition. But if it's malnutrition, I kept inquiring, how will you cure it by food stamps—which are simply cash in the grocery stores. Hardin never gave a meaningful answer.

Nixon believed defiantly that there was no hunger problem in America; that the problem was being fabricated by journalists and politicians; and that the whole anti-hunger campaign was a hoax and disgrace. He said so more than once in my meetings with him.

He also took a stand against enlarging the food stamp program in fiscal 1970. Hardin pleaded that we proceed, as did Finch, Moynihan, et al. But the President was firm; we'll do it in fiscal 1971, not now, the budget will simply not allow it.

But the President was worried. Ehrlichman and others kept telling him that Congress was getting ready to spend several billion to fight hunger. How could the President hold back? Maybe there was no problem, they argued; but, since the Democrats here kicked up so much dust, people now believe there is, and they expect action.

Then came the day of reckoning—or rather the day before this; that is, Finch and Hardin had to testify the next day. What should they say? Would not the President, and his Administration, and they, and who not—be terribly embarrassed if they had no anti-hunger program to present? Fact that President had already decided the issue did not count with them; they had already discovered that the President was flexible, particularly when politics was a factor. So they pressed several of us; and good Mayo, kindly and wanting to be cooperative, announced he could transfer some 250 million from the military budget to the food stamps. My own part, too, was greatly cooperative; I did not object to Mayo's suggestion. Hardin and Finch seized on it. Ehrlichman went down to get the President's approval; he came back in a few minutes, beaming.

That's how the food program was launched. But next day I got thinking: Was this 250 (or was it 170 or 270) million the full annual cost? Something inside of me told me it might not be the full-year cost.

I checked and discovered the full-year cost would be over 1 billion.

Then called Mayo; he too didn't know that full-year cost would be something other than we had agreed to. A quick note of explanation to the President followed; clearly if we didn't know what we were doing, neither did he. But it was too late to reverse gears.

What stands out about the food stamp plan: (1) President talked about hunger problem when he didn't believe it existed (2) President wavered and then decided to "lead" the anti-hunger parade (3) Neither he nor his cabinet except Hardin, who knew but was too devoted to the cause of food stamps that he failed to enlighten us about cost, as he should have [saw this] (4) The food stamp plan was adopted, though I pointed out repeatedly that it was not an anti-hunger program, nor an anti-malnutrition program; that it was simply a scheme for redistribution of income, although not an efficient redistribution scheme; and that it would be desirable to wait with the food stamps until we could see how the new welfare program would go, and how—if at all—the food stamp plan would fit in.

The recently announced welfare reform was to do away with food stamps (in order to keep down costs); but then it was discovered—the President didn't know this—that the recent welfare benefit plus promised food stamps would yield larger benefits to many than new welfare plan. This came as a shock to administration (certainly to President & Ehrlichman; and to Moynihan who cares neither for truth nor public money), and at once the cry went up that nobody would be worse off. The additional cost, on account of the food stamp fiasco, is still being computed. It will probably be a billion or so.

[Fiscal 1970 was July 1, 1969–June 30, 1970.]

1969 **1970** 1971 1972 1973 1974

Perhaps it was just as well that Burns allowed his diary virtually to lapse for much of this second year of the administration. To be sure, he did not have much to say, beyond the fact that he was pulling together the organization of the Fed, changing the looseness that had characterized the Martin regime. The president announced his nomination in October 1969, Burns took office in January, and for months thereafter he was busy. When he did write it was to relate his uncertainty about the important personalities he was working with. For some lesser sorts he could be certain. He threw darts at the two principals of the California contingent on the White House staff, H. R. (or Bob, as he almost grudgingly described him) Haldeman and John Ehrlichman. They were messengers, and unnecessary, for on most of the messages they carried the contents should have been related by the president, by telephone or interview. Moreover, the messengers were inept; one could not be sure the messages were correct; the presidential words might be garbled.

Burns was uncertain, however, about three of the more important personalities. He wondered about the staying power of Secretary of the Treasury Kennedy. Rumor was about that Kennedy could not last. But this was in an administration full of gossip and surmise and backbiting. Burns knew that just because he, the chairman, was straightforward and forceful, the rumormongers were saying critical things about himself.

During these months he also worried about the instincts and purposes of George Shultz, whom he eventually came to see was thoroughly honest. His initial concern about the Urban Affairs Council, the Moynihan "spenders," made him sensitive to anyone who did not seem to want to balance the budget and do everything possible to avoid inflation; stagflation for Burns meant measures against inflation. Sometimes Shultz took tactical detours from Burns's ideas and the Fed chairman did not recognize them as such.

The last of Burns's uncertainties concerned the rise to cabinet status, secretary of the treasury, of the then Democrat and former governor of Texas,

John Connally. President Nixon first asked Burns if Burns would like the treasury. It seemed a great compliment but Burns decided in favor of the independence he had at the Fed. Nixon perhaps knew he would choose the Fed and advanced an offer Burns would not take; the diary does not speculate on this possibility. The result, however, was the designation of Connally, for the Fed chairman an inconvenient mixture of talents. Charming when he wished to be, able to move his thoughts from "A" to "B" or wherever else, as logic demanded, which meant a clear thinker, he knew nothing of economics and did not especially want to learn. Highly political, he knew that the president was the arbiter of cabinet thoughts and had to be catered to; Connally would jump whatever way the president desired, not necessarily choosing what was best for the country. (Robert Solomon, Burns's principal staff adviser on international economics, heard from a colleague that Connally possessed "no idealism." Solomon, *The International Monetary System: 1945–1981* [New York: Harper and Row, 1982], 191.) To all this Connally added a dislike of foreigners that tempted him to insult them in international meetings. The business of inflating the currency would prove awkward enough for Burns, requiring as much foreign cooperation as possible. Connally, despite his domestic talents, was no assistance beyond the water's edge.

Nov. 7 Although deeply moved and delighted by President's suggestion that I assume the post of Sec'y of Treasury around the year-end, I had the good sense to give an uncommitted reply, suggest that we talk about this after the election, that I would in the meanwhile search my own mind and also the availability of other candidates.

In presenting the problem, the President made an accurate appraisal of Kennedy and Walker. Kennedy is a well-meaning, decent man, but he lacks energy and imagination. Walker has plenty of both, but is short on character. The President was a little harsh in judging McCracken; the difficulty with him is not on the advisory side but in his weakness as a leader. Once that is recognized, he can serve admirably; but this also means that he must make fewer speeches and no longer serve as chairman of cabinet *action* committees.

I've just about reached conclusion to remain where I am despite the extra prestige that goes with the Treasury post. If this had been offered to me at the outset, I would have taken it—gladly and viewed it as fulfillment. Now, things are different. First, I am in the midst of a crucially important job, I'm handling it well despite great odds, I've got many things started that I want to see through, and I want to stay long enough to leave a permanent mark. Second, I like my independence, and I have it here in a degree that I could not enjoy at the Treasury. I could probably handle the Haldemans and the Ehrlichmans efficiently enough; but I choke when I think of some of the legislation that I might have to support or the politically twisted speeches that I might be forced into. Still the Treasury post fascinates me for its range of opportunity; and maybe I am influenced also by some signs of declining energy of late—but I think not.

Hauge and Bob Leech are the two best names so far. The first is politically wise and has good character. I think he also has a well-balanced mind and good economic sense. The second is much tougher on matters of finance, and less inclined to compromise—which may be why I prefer him, but I recognize the risks—particularly since I know him less well than Hauge. I must think hard and pray!

[Gabriel Hauge had been President Eisenhower's administrative assistant for economic affairs. Leech, as related below, was with J. P. Morgan Guaranty Bank.]

Nov. 23 I saw the President on Friday, November 20th. The ¾ hour reported by the Pres. was actually 1¾ hours. The confrontation reported or predicted by the press did not come off. Nor did I think it would. The President knows his limitations in the economic area; and while the sycophants around the White House, whose numbers have been multiplying, keep talking about the money supply and the excessive caution of the Fed, the President knows that I know my economics and that he has much to learn from me and that I am not ready to be either his pupil or his functionary. The President merely asked two or three questions about money & credit, and we spent the time on what he should be doing *not* on what the Fed should or should not do.

Before turning to economic policy, I told the President that I had come to decision on the Treasury post, that I had started something at the Fed that was of importance to me and to the country, and that it would be wasteful for me to move so quickly to another post. I went on to say that I had considered carefully who Kennedy's successor might be and that my present list included three names—Hauge, Williams of IBM, and Ralph Leech of J P Morgan – Guaranty. The President indicated that he understood my position and that he would not press in view of my feelings; that Williams lacked color and political appeal. He was silent on Hauge, inquired closely about Leech, and seemed fearful; after I described the toughness of his mind and character that he would not bend sufficiently to political necessity. He then put forward a suggestion of his own—Anderson of Atlantic Richfield and asked me to make inquiries about him and let him know. He left me with the feeling that Kennedy might stay on another few months, perhaps indefinitely. But I doubt that he will; he is obviously of little or no benefit to the Administration; and he will be a natural scapegoat when the failures of Administration economic policy become so clear that even Shultz and McCracken may find their theology slipping from under them.

The inadequacies of Administration economic policy constituted my main and quite impersonal theme. What the boys that swarm around the White House fail to see is that the country now faces an entirely new problem—namely, a sizable inflation in the midst of recession; that classical remedies for fighting inflation or recession will simply not do; that new medicine is needed for the new illness; that more rapid expansion of the money supply cannot be the answer since there is [not] a shortage of money but a certain hesitation or [un]willingness to use it; that confidence needs to be restored; that this can be done by a two-pronged policy, first, through fiscal reforms such as accelerated depreciation and the value-added tax with appropriate reduction of income tax, second, through a long and necessary series of actions designed to improve the structure and functioning of markets, particularly the labor market; and that this market-oriented range of policies—popularly labeled "incomes policy"—is absolutely necessary to shorten the transitioning phase, in which we are now caught, of moving from cost-push inflation to economic balance. The President instructed Ehrlichman to proceed promptly on accelerated depreciation and the value-added tax, and to explore each of my ten proposals for incomes policy. I emphasized that time is short, that he will eventually have to adapt to incomes policy, that events will force such a move, that the chances for his success in 1972 would be best if he moved promptly, and that I cared not at all whether he took my suggestions or some others—provided he went about this seriously and avoided cosmetics.

One thing that the President told me, which impressed me greatly, was that he had decided to scrap *all* grant-in-aid programs, to substitute a grand revenue sharing program for the miscellany of specific grants, and to add 5 billion to the sum. I congratulated him and went away deeply encouraged that at least some of the things I have sweated over may come to fruition. If the President really goes through with this—though I remain doubtful about his doing so—he will bring honor to himself and new hope to the country.

["Accelerated depreciation" required Congress to enact an investment tax credit, allowing companies to deduct a certain percentage of capital spending from their tax bill—effectively subsidizing investment. In the above-mentioned possibilities for ending stagflation Burns mentioned the value-added tax, an unaccustomed tax for Americans, although not for Europeans. The VAT, or consumption tax, affects goods and services and goes by percentages, in each case subtracting tax already paid. In 2009 the burgeoning federal debt caused by the economic meltdown of 2008 revived thoughts of the VAT as a quick way to reduce the national debt and the *New York Times* of December 11 gave the example of a dress: the fabric cost $10 (tax $1), sewing $30 (tax $3, with $1 subtracted), retail $50 (tax $5, $3 subtracted).

For incomes policy, see pages 34–35.

Albert L. Williams was former president of IBM. Robert O. Anderson was the founder of Atlantic Richfield Oil Company.]

Nov. 24 Had a busy day again, like every day at the Fed so far. A board meeting, talks with Patman, Senator Bennett, Speaker McCormack, two newspapermen, etc. But what interested me most was George Shultz. When I told him that all that the stories about the Fed's conflict with the Administration were doing was to build up future trouble for the Administration and that the White House children ought to stop the dangerous game of feeding gossip and fabrications to the press, he agreed fully with me and expressed his disgust and dismay. Later in the day, the fellow from *Newsweek* named Shultz as the chief formulator of such news stories. Shultz is able, but is he honest? Does he have character? For some time, my doubts have been accumulating, as I watch his thinking—which runs consistently along political lines even when the truth needs to be strained. But I never thought of him as a calculating manipulator, and I must watch more closely before I [allow] my opinion to harden.

[Wright Patman was Democratic congressman from Texas; Wallace Bennett was Republican senator from Utah; and John W. McCormack was Democratic congressman from Massachusetts.]

Dec. 20 President called on Monday, December 14, at 11:15 a.m. and informed me that he was appointing Connally as Sec. of Treasury and that the announcement would be made publicly in another 15 minutes. He explained that he had decided against Anderson, although I had not yet reported about him. The reason for doing this was increasing realization that Congress would become bitterly partisan, that the appointment of a Democrat would help to keep things under control, that Connally could work effectively with the Congress, and that his skill was needed to get new programs across—including, as it would, such controversial items as liberalized depreciation and the value-added tax.

This news came as a shock to me. Why Connally? I stammered out a question: Does he [know] anything about Federal finances or interactive finances? Clearly, as I realized the very moment I popped the question, it was stupid then, with the decision made, to voice the doubts. But I must have been just speaking to myself, as a person in a state of shock often will. But the President took me seriously; he clearly was nervous and on the defensive. He explained that Connally must know something about finance since he is serving as a director of the U.S. Trust Co. in New York and also a large Houston bank. As for the rest, the President explained, he would learn from me as the President himself had done and was doing. In any event, the President went on, he needed Connally—a strong and influential man—for practical reasons. The President also remarked that the only ones who then knew of the appointment were Kennedy, Connally, Bill Rogers and myself. Next and finally, the President indicated that he was sending Connally over for a talk promptly, and that I should be as helpful as I could to him. I promised I would and wished him well.

Kennedy came over for lunch, and he filled my heart with sadness. He learned about the Connally decision the preceding Friday, argued against it on ground that Connally lacked experience, but to no avail, President offered him a post as Ambassador-at-large, with responsibilities in international financial area; he could, moreover, retain a seat in Cabinet and serve as adviser. Some two weeks previously, as I understood Kennedy, he had offered to resign; but the President then refused to consider it. Apparently the President had changed his mind suddenly, once he determined just whom he wanted for the Kennedy post.

Kennedy showed full understanding that the ambassadorial post was probably created to put a good face on the shift in command; he wondered whether he really ought to take the new job when it was not clear that he would have a real job to handle; but that he agreed anyhow to do so, expecting to drop out quietly later if it became clear that his services were not needed or ignored—if needed. I agreed with this course of action, but did not tell him—all the more so because he nearly broke my heart—what the President and I had been discussing for some months.

I urged Kennedy to leave a strong and permanent legacy, and that he could do so by joining me in insistence on a budget that would fall a little short of 225 billion rather than exceed it; also, for prompt liberalized depreciation; for revision of income tax structure, with value added tax replacing part of personal & corporate income tax; for scrapping of categorical grants or at least a very sharp reduction, combined with a *huge* revenue sharing plan. Kennedy agreed to work hard for a responsible fiscal program, and it will be interesting to see if he can do so. I hope he can.

Connally came over in mid-afternoon. We talked for about ¾ hour. I had met him previously. Once & again, I was impressed by the clarity and vigor of his rhetoric. I was impressed also by his "conservatism," his dislike of big government, his contempt for trade unions. But I got no clue to the questions that were agitating me: Is Connally a spender like Johnson, despite his "conservatism"? What are his views on tax policy? What he knew about international finance—a matter of greatest importance in view of the probable proximity of a monetary upheaval? Does he know about the traditions of the Fed & will he respect its independence? I tried not to press Connally; merely conveyed my concern about [the] sorry state of the economy & expressed hope that he and I would work closely together.

Before Connally left I was sure that I would like him; and I also realized that the next few weeks would tell whether Connally—who is not scheduled to take over until Feb. 1—will be major architect of fiscal policy or simply the President's salesman in this area (and probably others—military & foreign policy).

[William P. Rogers was secretary of state.]

Dec. 29 Have just concluded a week of pure rest in St. Thomas, and then for a brief stop in Palm Beach and back to Washington. My mind keeps running back to Dec. 21 when the President gathered the Cabinet and all his appointees for a meeting in the East Room. Rogers spoke first, and gave an excellent account of our achievements in foreign policy since the election of 1968. I think that Rogers has matured richly on the job; he speaks with more confidence, comes to the point quickly and effectively, and, what is most important, speaks good sense and with a dignity that I did not expect of him.

Shultz spoke next, on domestic policy, and he continues to disappoint me. I expected much of him as Sec'y of Labor, and that is why I recommended him for the post and plumped so hard for him. I would not have picked him for the Budget post, because that post requires a man of firm principles rather than a genius for mediation; but George lacks the former, while he has the latter in superabundance. As I watch George, I'm troubled increasingly by his political approach to his own duties; but that is probably the very quality that endears him to the President. I wonder whether George does not have political ambitions of his own. Kennedy suggested to me not long ago that George wanted to be Vice President. Absurd? I no longer think so. I could not help but wince when George concluded. His empty recite of domestic achievements with an extended panegyric of the President's marvelous leadership. George is not stupid; he could not have meant half of what he said. Yet I also noticed that the President beamed as George delivered his song of praise. I think that George knows his man and is using him. But what of the President? He doubtless finds George's love of compromise, his reluctance to hurt any political group, most congenial. Does he also realize that George's sense of expediency, combined with the amoral leanings of Ehrlichman and Haldeman, may result in his undoing? Probably not. My immediate concern is the budget, and I am afraid that George has no sense of responsibility in this area. I hope I am wrong.

The final speaker was Moynihan. It was a relief to listen to him after Shultz. Pat is wonderfully articulate and lends charm even to trite phrases—which are fewer in his case than in that of any member of Nixon's staff or Cabinet. He, too, however, knows Nixon's weaknesses; & he used the occasion to shower praise on Nixon on a scale that made Shultz's earlier panegyric seem most grudging. While I think Moynihan misled the President badly on the welfare problem, something will be lost when he is gone. After listening to Pat on this occasion, I'm no longer sure that he will publish his book on the Nixon administration in 1970—just in time to disclose to the nation what Nixon really thinks about the school problem, the Negro, etc. Perhaps Moynihan has more decency than I previously thought; but I still wonder how & when he is going to use the full notes he took of what the President & everyone else said at every meeting. Time will tell!

My mind goes back also to the Pepperdine speech I gave in L.A. on December 7—a Monday. I kept working on the speech through the morning of Saturday, December 5. Finally, the typing and Xeroxing was finished by 3:30. In another hour I was to leave for the plane & therefore began gathering my papers for the trip. While so occupied, the phone rings and Catherine announces that the President wanted to speak to me. My heart sank; for I knew at once that he would want to advise me how to proceed at Pepperdine. And so it was! The President began by talking about Bill Martin who wanted to attract attention; that he was sure I would not want to air my differences with him in public, and that I should realize that he will move further towards an incomes policy in due course. I explained that I was fully sensitive to the need of avoiding any impression of a conflict between us; and that he could judge for himself by listening, if he so wished, to the two or three pages of my speech devoted to incomes policy. The President expressed the wish and I read rapidly (and somewhat nervously), but he seemed pleased when I finished; at least, he said he was. And, indeed, he should have been; for I practiced great restraint in the Pepperdine precisely because I wanted to avoid loose talk about a confrontation, etc.

The reason I was so sure that it was the President calling was simple: Bill Safire called the day before, offered to advise me on my speech and expressed the President's concern. What a shame that the President's staff keeps worrying him so uselessly!

[The journalist William L. Safire was special assistant to the president.

Incomes policy was the burden of Burns's speech at Pepperdine College in California. It was one of his efforts to deal with stagflation and, however carefully, it ran up against the president's crude solution, as Burns would have put it, which opted for an increase in the money supply (to assist reelection in 1972). Burns as Fed chairman had to consider several subtleties in the state of the nation's economy. Part of the trouble was the slowing down of business activity. Unemployment was rising beyond the figure that might have been seen as normal, containing workers who did not wish to hold jobs. At the same time—the novelty—there was inflation. Labor unions were taking advantage of any monopolistic position they held; the construction unions obtained a 15 percent increase in wages in 1970. At the end of the year the unions at General Motors subjected the corporation to a long strike. Other unions were bound to follow these examples. The Fed chairman by no means was against unions but naturally was trying to hold down their demands. Inflation in 1970 was 5.7 percent, nearly as much as in 1969. Profit margins were very thin and the only way corporations could increase wages was to raise prices. Incomes policy would call for a freeze on wages and prices. It had worked in the Kennedy administration. To be sure, to champion what might be labeled as a Democratic policy was inconvenient for a Republican administration. Burns himself did not like the idea but did not think he could advocate anything else—the VAT was politically nearly impossible. To offer corporations tax incentives to increase investment was likely not to produce enough results to make right the economy's stagflation. Wyatt C. Wells, *Economist in an Uncertain World: Arthur F. Burns and the Federal Reserve, 1970–78* (New York: Columbia University Press, 1994).]

1969 1970 **1971** 1972 1973 1974

The Rubicon of Arthur Burns's two terms as chairman of the Federal Reserve Board was 1971 when it became thoroughly evident to administration insiders and for that matter many outsiders, although they lacked certitude, that the Nixon administration would opt out of stagflation by what Burns believed was a cheap alternative—cheap in the sense of being easy, as opposed to taking a responsible course. They would inflate the currency unduly and give a temporary advantage, enough to get through the president's reelection—by cheapening American manufactures against those of foreign nations. One says "inflate the currency unduly." The crisis that was approaching was the need to inflate, for the dollar was too high, manufactures were too high in foreign markets, competition had become too keen. The dollar needed cheapening. Just how much no one knew, least of all Burns. That was the problem in adjustment. He knew that the president was likely to resort to more inflation than was necessary to right the position of American manufactures in world markets, and that John Connally, secretary of the treasury, would go along with this plan.

The secondary danger in the necessary cheapening of the dollar was that the administration, closing the gold window while it raised the price of gold (cheapening the dollar), would not open the window again. The notion of a float of the dollar carried its own attraction, for it seemed to assure Adam Smith's unseen hand, the autonomy of the free market. After all, a float was better than sinking the currency, whatever that might entail apart from the metaphor. But to Burns the need for opening the window, once the dollar floated, was to maintain the ability to exchange currency for gold, which made fooling with currencies more difficult, hence tended to prevent it. The United States had sponsored the Bretton Woods agreements of 1944 for that good purpose. Nixon and Connally apparently cared little for the international order in currency, Connally likely to take any swipe at the foreigners.

In the longer term the point of interest, politically, not so evident at the time, was that the Republican president would have no difficulty in the election of 1972, therefore no special economic measures were necessary. There was working here a fear of defeat that Burns believed was churned up by "the boys" in the White House, symbolized by the California messengers Haldeman and Ehrlichman. In fact it was a fear originating from the president himself.

The Davis-Bacon Act, with which the entry of March 8, 1971, begins, dealt with wage floors for federal contractors. The Quadriad comprised the chairman of the Federal Reserve Board, the chairman of the Council of Economic Advisors, the director of the OMB, and secretary of the treasury, with the president sitting in.

March 8 The President finally acted on Davis-Bacon—a year and a half late, but still a courageous decision. That it happened at all is itself a good sign, for it means that Shultz's influence—a pernicious and stultifying force—is waning.

The Quadriad meeting on Friday, March 5, was a startling and even frightening performance. The President looked wild; talked like a desperate man; fulminated with hatred against the press; took some of us to task—apparently meaning me or McCracken or both—for not putting a gay and optimistic face on every piece of economic news, however discouraging; propounded the theory that confidence can be best generated by appearing confident and coloring, if need be, the news; explained that he did that in foreign affairs and that we ought to do same in economic matters; Connally—a most smooth politician—nodded charmingly from time to time; Shultz—always a good boy—did not say a word; poor McCracken was visibly frightened—too frightened to speak out; only I spoke out, explaining that McCracken could not get away with prevarication—all of which released a torrent of resentment against me: my wanting to be independent, to make a name for myself, to preach about incomes policies—all of which can only endanger the Administration—and do me no permanent good. I am not really sure that he said all of this; he was incoherent much of the time; and when I reminded him that my pronouncements on incomes policy had his prior, although perhaps, not his enthusiastic, approval, he responded quickly that he didn't mind that, that he didn't have that in mind. Apparently, the President was stung by my pronouncement at a Congressional hearing that what the economy suffered from was a shortage of confidence rather than a shortage of money.

I am convinced that the President will do anything to be reelected. The sad thing is that by throwing all principles to the wind, he is rapidly reducing his chances for reelection. The harassing of the Fed by the President and his pusillanimous staff will continue and may even intensify. Fortunately, although I am no longer sure whether the President fully knows this, I am still his best friend. By standing firm, I will serve the economy—and thereby also the President—best.

There were moments during this meeting when I felt that the President was going mad. But there were also moments of warm and touching friendship, as when he reminded me of our conversation about the SST over a year ago. I then told him why I advise, on economic grounds, against continuing; whereupon, he proceeded to discourse on America's mission and destiny, that a great nation seeking to extend its greatness could not govern itself by economic rules only, that forces of science and technology should not be kept back, that the SST would lead America in the forefront of aeronautics, where it indeed must be, etc. I was deeply moved at the time, and said to the President, "That's the way I love my President to speak." I meant this most sincerely, and I was touched by the fact that it meant so much to him that he now recalled it, wondering whether I remembered. This episode, and his invitation to Pat's party on the 16th, saved the day for me; but I left with a deeply troubled mind.

Today, after church services, I whispered to the President that I must see him privately. Meetings during the past several months have finally convinced me that the ignoramuses around the White House, led by the fanatical Shultz, have just about convinced the President that monetary policy is not what it should be. I'll do what I can to set him straight, because I hate to see him worry so unnecessarily about matters that he neither understands nor can do anything about.

[The above passage of Burns's diary is one of the most pathetic—not for the diarist but for the president—passages of the entire Nixon years. Here one has exactly what the consummate political writer Elizabeth Drew wrote at the conclusion of her sketch of President Nixon in *Richard M. Nixon*, the series of presidential sketches edited by the late Arthur M. Schlesinger, Jr. (New York: Times Books, 2007), 149–151. Ms. Drew could not say for certain that this president was ill, for there were flashes of wisdom at even his most desperate moments—one of which Burns wrote about in the above entry. But the analyst of many an administration, seeking to understand 1969–1974, could not be sure any account would work without resort to medicine—President Nixon's was no normal personality.

The SST was an economic white elephant. The reference to "Pat" is to Mrs. Nixon. President and Mrs. Nixon held a dinner for Prime Minister and Mrs. John Lynch of Ireland, an "Irish party" at which they announced the engagement of their daughter Tricia.]

March 21 I saw RN on Friday, March 19. Ten days earlier I had whispered to him at Sunday services that I wanted a private meeting. He remembered this and told me he would arrange it—this he did at meeting with Lord Cromer. My eagerness to see [him] stemmed from an eagerness to have a candid talk about the war of nerves that the White House gang had set in motion. Recently, a journalist came to see me and told me that some WH operatives (specifically, Haldeman & Shultz) had their bayonets out for me. Connally came to see me on Thursday, March 18, said same thing, and advised that I see the President. I told him that I had already reached the decision to do this.

I informed the President as follows: (1) that his friendship was one of the three that has counted most in my life and that I wanted to keep it if I possibly could; (2) that I took the present post to repay the debt of an immigrant boy to a nation that had given him the opportunity to develop and use his brains constructively; (3) that there was never the slightest conflict between my doing what was right for the economy and my doing what served the political interests of RN; (4) that if a conflict ever arose between these objectives, I would not lose a minute in informing RN and seeking a solution together; (5) that the sniping in the press that the WH staff was engaged in had not the slightest influence on Fed policy, since I will be moved only by evidence that what the Fed is doing is not serving the nation's best interests; (6) that the WH staff had created an atmosphere of confrontation which led to the exaggeration of said differences about economic policy as may exist between the Fed and the Administration; that (7) squabbling or the appearance of squabbling among high government officers could lead to a weakening of confidence in government policy and thereby injure the prospects of economic improvement.

RN seemed pleased by my reassurances to him, indicated that he never had any doubts, that he would put an end promptly to the sniping about the Fed that has been going on at the White House, that he agreed with my policy, that he preferred a slow start of the recovery which may then gather momentum in 1972, that he wants to rely primarily on me and Connally in monitoring policy, that McCracken and Shultz—while able economists—did not understand politics, that I could handle both economics and politics, and that Connally was good at politics and therefore a great asset.

[Lord Cromer was head of the Bank of England.]

April 12 President made good on his promise. This I heard from Ehrlichman and Shultz. The sniping has ended—at least for the present. Indeed, Shultz—now trying to be a good boy and to prove it—is going out of his way to say nice things about me and the Fed, and making sure that I get the report on his sayings.

May 4 Before going off to Basle, I saw RN on Frid. My main purpose was to get him to approve a statement I wanted to make to central bank governors: first, that the President's as determined as ever to fight inflation; second, that he will not tolerate any further mischief from those who preach the doctrine of "benign neglect" of balance of payments. RN agreed readily, as I knew he would. I also urged the President to reconsider his objection to a price and wage review board; that something like this was necessary to prevent a sharp rise of wages and prices of steel; that the Cabinet Committee on Ec. Policy could serve as his wage and price review board; that it could perform this function on the principle of an accordion, expanding or contracting in activity as he deemed best. This seemed of real interest to him and he promised to study the idea.

We also discussed monetary policy and why I thought some prompt increase of short-term interest rates was essential—for domestic as well as international reasons.

Connally's performance came up. I praised him to the sky, pointed to his charisma, his loyalty to RN, his effectiveness with people. President asked me how C. compared with other cabinet members. My reply was prompt: he is head and shoulders above everyone there, that the other members of the Cabinet were dull and a dubious asset to him, by and large; that Connally was a brilliant discovery. President thereafter noted that he let Kennedy go after he learned my opinion about his leadership ability, that he agrees with my judgment about both Kennedy and Connally, and that he wanted very much to know which of the present members of the Cabinet were of presidential timber. It's all Connally was my single reply; he and he alone. President agreed. John Ehrlichman, who was present at this meeting, echoed answer most eagerly; and I got the impression that this subject had come up before between RN and JE. In any event, the President agreed heartily with us both.

Meeting in Basle explained to governors that they were pursuing a dangerous policy in transferring dollars held in NY to the Eurodollar market; that, whether they did this directly or through the BIS, they created new dollar reserves; that their dollar reserves were multiplying in large measure because of their own action, not only—as is commonly claimed—as a result of US balance of payments; that while the transfer of dollars to the Eurodollar market was profitable to the central banks, their function was to police the monetary system, not to make profits; and that it is essential, therefore, to halt this mischievous exercise in finance. This practice was generally agreed to and a halting operation was decided upon.

Today's meeting of the Quadriad dealt with the new monetary crisis, arising from the influx of dollars into Germany—stimulated by loose talk of German politicians about revaluing the mark. Meeting went in zigzag fashion; but finally I got agreement on a statement to be issued to the press, reaffirming our adherence to a system of fixed parities—although this agreement came after rather than during our meeting with President. When I called Dr. Klassen and read statement to him, he expressed his great happiness over our act, informed me too that he was at odds with others in his government, that he had firmly concluded that he must resign if the government revalued, that our statement strengthened his position enormously, and that he now felt the mark would not be revalued. RN was pleased with the statement and also with Klassen's reaction. I hope that our action proves right. I wish I were certain that we're on the right track; but even if not, the path we elected will prove preferable to sheer indecision—this always erodes both the capacity for leadership and one's entitlement to it.

[Established by agreements at The Hague in 1930, the Bank for International Settlements serves as a bank for central banks. It is not accountable to governments. Karl Klassen was president of West Germany's Bundesbank.]

May 22 Today's Quadriad meeting was uneventful; but after meeting was over, I stopped to chat with President alone about Giscard d'Estaing's suggestion to me: namely, that the U.S. take the lead in rebuilding the international monetary order. In course of discussion with Giscard, he made it clear that he believed the dollar was overvalued, that revaluation of other currencies was essential, that France too would be willing to appreciate its currency somewhat (implying that its revaluation would need to be smaller than others), that some 5 major countries would do the conferring, and that conference could be completed in 3 days. These ideas are most congenial to me. Giscard did not mention the price of gold as an item to be negotiated; but he probably has [it] in mind. President liked my idea of determining just when we want to come out, then moving to bilateral conversations to determine views of others, and finally move to a 5 or 6 country weekend conference if it appeared that we could come close to getting what we felt we need and should have. To do this, we should be willing to accept an increase in the price of gold of, say, 15 to 25%; but this concession should not come quickly. President liked this entire approach—it was substantially what I had recommended to him in October 1968; and he urged me to move ahead on the plan and I shall try to do so.

My problem may be Connally, who is likely to stall and not move ahead. I continue to regard him as a great improvement on Kennedy. He is an able, clever, and enchanting man. But he is not the decisive man I thought he was. I have watched him closely of late in group meetings and what I find—with some frequency—is that he agrees with practically everyone, although entirely opposite theories or courses of action are being advanced. Sometimes this may be done due to lack of full understanding; but I rather doubt if that is the case. The more likely explanation is that Connally wants to be friendly with everyone—particularly the White House staff, and that he is willing to bend his views—at least momentarily—to cement his personal relationships. All this is thoroughly understandable on the part of a man who is still young, ambitious, and has so much going for him. Yet I keep wishing that the new Secretary of the Treasury would show some capacity for leadership and act more decisively. Can it be that, despite all appearances to the contrary, Connally is not really a leader? I have seen enough of him to know that he neither is, nor ever will be, an architect of ideas; but I do not deem that essential to a political leader. I often feel these days that Connally appears at his best when he espouses the President's program; he is very, very good at that, and this makes him a wonderful asset for the President. But is Connally the man we need in the White House?

Perhaps Connally will strike out more boldly once he has secured his position. That he is trying to do this is altogether clear, and the President is helping him as I have been doing. At this meeting the President announced that he wanted Connally to be a spokesman for the administration in economic matters and that he wanted procedures developed to achieve this end. It was clear that Connally put the President up to this. I hope that the new arrangement will work out; but I am skeptical.

It will be interesting to see Connally expand his authority. I doubt if he will attempt to move into my corner; but I cannot be sure. If he does,

I'm inclined to think that he will retreat quickly and ostensibly in good humor.

These reflections about Connally are in large part a result of our constant meetings over the international monetary crisis. So far, what he has done has been in my direction. Neither of the two statements he put out would have been issued if I had not urged them with some vigor. That Connally is going my way is reassuring to me; that [he] is doing so slowly and after considerable deliberation is to his credit; but I have not yet detected the capacity for leadership that I hope for in him. Perhaps the novelty of the subject is the obstacle to bolder expression, but he appears to behave similarly on other problems.

[Burns was unsure of how much of a leader Connally could be and then promptly gives Connally credit for the presidential suggestion that he, the secretary, should be the voice of the administration on fiscal issues. In fact, as soon became evident, the president wished a single voice on such policy, which was not to be the secretary's but that of the president himself. Valery Giscard d'Estaing was French finance minister.]

July 8 The White House called on Sunday, June 27, to set up an appointment with the President on Monday afternoon. I had expected this call, since the President knew that I wanted a private meeting with him—which he made clear to me, on his own initiative, at the receiving line on lovely Tricia's wedding. When I arrived at the W.H. on Monday and found Connally waiting for the same appointment, I knew that something was up. Some political meetings were held by the President in recent days, and I gathered that he probably had reached some decisions that he wanted to communicate to us both. In a matter of minutes, however, I discovered that Connally was there to give support to the President, that he knew precisely the purpose; and that both had a message for a request of me.

The President was obviously ill-at-ease, but he had rehearsed his part and knew what he must convey to me; first, that he had reached a decision against a Wage and Price Review Board, which I had repeatedly recommended; second, that he thought I had written an effective letter urging a new policy; but that he cannot accept the recommendation (he gave no reason, though I knew it from earlier conversation); third, that he had informed the Cabinet and others in the administration that everyone in the economic field must henceforth speak with one voice; fourth, that Connally would become the spokesman for the Administration (this had been decided weeks earlier and announced at a Quadriad meeting); fifth, that while my status was a special one, I too will be expected to conform to publicly announced Administration policies, that my advocacy or comments on non-monetary matters was being interpreted widely as Administration policy—because of my friendship with the President that everyone knew; sixth, that the President was tired of the mouthings of people who sought a footnote in history books, and that everyone should recognize that if the President is successful there will be enough praise for everyone—and that if he isn't the footnote in history, which some seemed so eager to realize, wouldn't count at all, since nothing of any value would be left in the United States once the Democrats returned to power. The last remarks, which were clearly intended for McCracken besides myself, bruised my spirit; partly because of the failure to understand the motives that governed honorable men in government, but even more because of the brutality of RN's language. I watched his face, as he spoke, with a feeling of dismay; for his features became twisted and what I saw was uncontrolled cruelty. I kept wondering, as he spoke, when he would stop; for I had a thing or two to say myself—and I felt strong enough to do it calmly and with compassion.

The President stopped in the course of his lengthy and nervous lecture to me to ask me a few specific questions—mainly, was I in favor of a wage and price freeze, to which I replied, "Not now. Let us first see if milder medicine will work"; also, was I in favor of a tax cut to which I simply replied "I would favor a reinstallment of the investment tax [credit]; but since Congress would do this only if income taxes were simultaneously cut, the tax relief would be excessive and I would prefer to do nothing in this area at present." These answers harmonized with the President's own thought; and his face brightened momentarily—much to my relief.

I was especially struck by the President's comment, which however was not entirely a surprise to me, that my advocacy of governmental actions, which he had not yet decided upon, made it difficult for him to come out for or take such actions; because he wanted novelty and excitement and a boldly innovative spirit to issue from the White House; and that when government officials, including myself, urged certain policies before he reached a decision, then when he later announced some such policies, they had already lost the dramatic punch they would have achieved if he was the first to make the pronouncement. His eyes blinked and his hands fidgeted as he made this confession; it was obviously painful to him to say all this so bluntly; but he obviously had resolved that I must know how he felt. I had long suspected that the President lacked true self-assurance, but I tried to wave these doubts aside. This I could no longer do as I listened to him; and while my heart was filled with sadness for him, I was seized suddenly with fear for the safety of our country which depended so heavily on this insecure man (the thought flashed through my mind of an earlier conversation, when he asked me to inform him when I thought it would be a good time to bring on an international monetary crisis and added, winking privately as he spoke, "I don't mind crises"—the I being heavily underlined).

I have not mentioned Connally, but I am indebted to him; for it was he who gave me the opportunity to reply, as I felt I must to the President. When Connally broke in at one point to repeat the essence of the President's argument and pointed to an article in the *N. Y. Times* which spoke approvingly of my Pepperdine speech, advising me that this is very bad and must stop, I seized upon his remarks to make my reply to the President which was simply this—that I had to testify on Wednesday, that I would undoubtedly be asked about the inflation and unemployment problems, that I would repeat my earlier views, that I would be acting out of character if I suddenly feigned ignorance, that I owed it to the Congress to speak my mind honestly, that I felt policies which I advocate would help the nation, and—though the President did not see it that way—they would really help him if they were adopted. It was then that the President pointed out that I am being regarded as a spokesman of the Administration; to which I replied that I doubted that very much; which caused the President to ask me to tell people that I wasn't, etc., etc. This part of the conversation seemed altogether pointless until the President informed me that if I espoused policies which he has rejected, the Washington community would interpret it as a breach between us. My reply was, and it came from the heart: "If that happened, it would be most unfortunate. I just want you to know I have always been your true friend, and I am that now and expect to remain so."

The day left me sad but I had no choice: Just as the President has his duties, so have I and I made this crystal clear to the President and to Connally. What surprised me was not the President's inner thoughts, but the contempt—which he articulated so fully—for other men who had minds of their own and a sense of conscience besides. Connally also surprised me. I thought that he was smart enough to know that there are some men in this world who refuse to play politics when this means disregard for one's oath of office or one's self-respect; and that I might be such a man. Nixon thought that he could appeal to my friendship and get his way; but Connally lacked this advantage or any other. I continue to like him and to admire his political skill; but he is less astute than I once thought he was. His willingness to echo whatever the President may be thinking may enhance his power for a time; but this power-hungry and most charming man, whatever fortune may hold out for him, will not be the kind of leader that this nation so badly needs and so richly deserves.

A memorable feature of this meeting with RN is that he simply informed me of his decision concerning the Wage and Price Review Board; he gave no reasons. Perhaps he omitted his reasoning, since he felt—and this would have been justifiable—that I knew his reasons. But I do not think this was the case. RN's entire manner was imperial; it was enough that he had reached a decision; that alone should govern the conduct of everyone in his Administration; that while mine, for constitutional reasons, was a very special case, he was still the emperor and I should therefore toe the mark—as should every good citizen, especially those who were or professed to be his friends. I had often noticed RN's love of the imperial manner and its trappings, but now I knew that I would be accepted in the future only if I suppressed my will and yielded completely—even though it was wrong at law and morally—to his authority.

[The emergence of the imperial presidency thus came, as the chairman of the Fed suddenly saw, in the year 1971. The charm of Connally remained, but behind what appeared to be a Connally initiative was the president, not the secretary. And within the imperial intention, according to Burns, was cruelty, as well as no understanding of what made democracy work, or at least had made democracy work in preceding administrations, in the United States of America.

For a historian after the many years, such as the accomplished Elizabeth Drew, all this gave a larger compass to the Nixon presidency than simply a medical explanation, which might have explained, among other things, the cruelty. It certainly placed issues beyond the personal and, for an immigrant boy such as Burns once had been, made everything unpatriotic.]

Aug. 12 On Aug. 5 RN telephoned. The day before he held a press conference, and finally—he took a long week to do so—scotched the slur on my good name that had been engineered by anonymous W.H. officials (actually, it was Shumway in Klein's office, serving as a tool for Colson); but for whom was Colson serving as a tool? Was it Haldeman, Ehrlichman or possibly, as many believe, RN himself? He explained that, quite contrary to the report in the press, I not only had not asked for a salary increase, but I had flatly refused it. RN said I did so because I felt it was wrong at a time of inflation. The explanation was good enough for me; though the fact is that I just refused—insisting that any increase was to accrue to my successor, not to me. RN said nothing about this foul leak coming from the White House; nor did he refer to the report, similarly leaked, that the membership of the Fed Board was to be raised from 7 to 14 and that the Fed was to be placed under the authority of W. House. All the same, RN's comment about me was generous and did clear up the offensive slur. In view of that I called him on Wednesday to express my appreciation.

He returned call on Thursday, explaining that his trip to N.Y. made it impossible to do so sooner. He assured me, on his own initiative, that he had not the slightest intention to change the structure of the Fed. He also stressed that our views on economics were not wide apart, that he opened the door to moving to an incomes policy (which he really did) during the press conference on Wednesday, that this was done deliberately, and that he might soon surprise me by moving on incomes policy. I, in turn, put a proposal for his consideration—to appoint a Commission, to report in 60 or 90 days, consisting of business leaders, labor leaders, public members, administration representatives, and—most important of all—the majority and minority leaders in Congress (Mansfield, Albert, Scott & Ford), this committee being charged with the task of developing a wage and price policy that could count on broad support. President indicated real interest, wondered whether the report could not come in 30 days, but was not sure that Mansfield & Albert would serve. I pointed out that if he [they] didn't, RN could excoriate them as hypocrites. We agreed to discuss this fully after the President returned from Maine.

Since then it has become even clearer than before that the sense across the entire nation condemned the ugly White House leak, that the moment for a wage-and-price policy had been greatly strengthened, but—unfortunately—that the stupidity and clumsiness of the White House mischief makers had outraged financial opinion the world over, and that an international monetary crisis of grim proportions had been hastened.

My efforts to prevent closing of the gold window—working through Connally, Volcker, and Shultz—do not seem to have succeeded. The gold window may have to be closed tomorrow because we now have a government that seems incapable, not only of constructive leadership, but of any action at all. What a tragedy for mankind!

[The pressure from the White House was difficult to handle, as was keeping the gold window open. The increasing wealth of the European nations and Japan and other factors had sent dollars out of control, and sent them as well to foreign countries where they could be sent back to the United States to purchase gold at $35 an ounce, too cheap a price; there were seven dollars outside the country for every dollar's worth of gold in Fort Knox. The West German government revalued the mark; the British government wanted to convert $750 million into gold. For the first time the United States was running trade deficits; though they would seem ridiculously small in later years, they were deficits nonetheless, reminding individuals with historical knowledge that the nation had run trade surpluses since 1896.

In addition there was the stagflation to address. Burns wanted an incomes policy, attaching wage increases to increases in labor productivity.

At the Camp David meeting of the administration's economic officials the international economic scene required attachment to the domestic economic scene. Among changes in what became Phase I of the president's New Economic Policy (a label too reminiscent of Lenin's NEP in 1921 to survive for long) the principal move internationally, apart from closing the gold window, the latter perhaps temporarily, was a 10 percent surcharge on imports, and domestically it was an investment tax credit of 10 percent and a ninety-day freeze on wages and prices.

Devan L. Shumway was in the office of communications for the executive branch. Charles W. Colson was special counsel to the president. Mike Mansfield of Montana was majority leader of the Senate, Carl Albert of Oklahoma was majority leader of the House. Hugh D. Scott of Pennsylvania was minority leader of the Senate, and Gerald R. Ford of Michigan was minority leader of the House.]

Aug. 22 The meeting at Camp David last weekend was not much of a surprise for me. On Aug. 4th the President opened the door to a new wage and price policy—not widely, to be sure, but he at least indicated that he might take another look. On Aug. 5th, when we talked over the phone, he stated—on his own initiative—that our differences were confined to the problem of wages and prices; that even on that subject we were not necessarily far apart—indeed, that he might surprise me one of these days. Whereupon I told Helen [Burns] that I expected the President to order a wage and price freeze; my reasoning being, first, that the President loved to think of himself—as he also would have others think—that he is a bold innovator, second, that I (and others) had not urged a freeze publicly—thereby augmenting the chances of such a move being regarded as highly innovative, dramatic, etc.

The meeting was also not much of a surprise for me because Shultz had come over with an urgent message—namely, that the President was thinking of making some major pronouncement on economic policy in the near future, and that the President wanted my views on the subject of wages & prices, taxes, gov't spending, and balance of payments, etc. Shultz was obviously the messenger and no more in this instance; he listened intently to what I had to say on these subjects, repeated my views more than once to make sure that he would be reporting accurately; and as the next day proved, he reported my thoughts fully and accurately to the President—for the President summarized my views at the very start of the discussions on Friday.

Thursday evening Shultz called and informed me of the plans for the weekend—we would leave in the early afternoon of Friday and be "locked up" at Camp David through Sunday. The departure was to be from the helicopter pad at the Pentagon; but Dwight Chapin called Friday morning to say that we would leave from the White House grounds. The President joined several of us from the helicopter; it was the first time I had seen him since the day when he and Connally launched their assault to quiet me. If there was any feeling of anger or annoyance still lurking in the President's mind, he did not show it—either then or at any time at Camp David. On the contrary, he was particularly deferential to my views; not only that, he kept referring to our old friendship, to this or that experience we had shared together, etc. Yet, he was concerned about my views; for both Shultz and Safire told me that he kept wondering whether I would go along with the decisions that had to be reached.

This first meeting was long, but peaceful and harmonious—as such things go. The President set the tone of earnestness and decisiveness; decisions would be reached; their effect would depend on complete secrecy; no telephone calls were to be made; any leak would be treason. The drama of all this was excessive; but it helped to put everyone into a constructive mood.

It became clear very quickly that the President would set out a tough wage and price policy, & that the only things to settle on were the details of that policy; also that he would move on taxes and on expenditures—the idea of setting the investment tax credit at 10% the first year and then going to 5 appealed to him and he seized it eagerly; the border tax was also on his mind as he wanted to move on that; but he was puzzled about what to do about the convertibility of dollars into gold and this subject was discussed more extensively than any other.

I argued that if RN adopted a tough wage and price policy, and also took steps to curb the proportion of percent, the import duty surcharge would be sufficient to bring about a rather prompt and sizable readjustment of exchange rates in our favor (something that Giscard d'Estaing and more lately the Japanese ambassador had assured me would happen). I expressed fear that a closing of gold window would lead to chaotic financial markets, and that it might be followed by trade wars, currency wars, and political friction—such as occurred during the thirties. No one else embraced this argument; they all seemed to want a floating exchange rate—either permanently, as in Shultz's case, or for some vague purpose or period, as with Connally and Volcker.

In the end, those who wanted to end convertibility had their way. The President's reasoning on this was interesting. If we left the window open and then realigned the exchange rates, the new arrangement might prove ephemeral and blow up next year before the election. To be sure, the immediate response—both here and abroad—would be unfavorable, but it was better to take the criticism now than later. The President explained that he had a way of dealing with crises, as in the case of the invasion of Laos; that is, taking a tough decision, accepting immediate criticism, but reaping the harvest of approval later on. So it would be also with the gold matter under discussion. All this seemed to assume—though nothing was said to this effect—that the dollar would be allowed to float until after the election. When I later pointed this out to Volcker, he became truly frightened and he has been doing penance for his recommendation to close the gold window—ever since.

There was extensive discussion also of the direct controls on direct investment and lending abroad. Connally advocated abandoning this, so did Shultz and others. I objected on two grounds: first, that the action would be interpreted as a belligerent move on our part to achieve maximum depreciation of the dollar; second, that the trade unionists would condemn the policy on the ground that we were fostering an accelerated export of the jobs of our people. The latter argument proved pervasive; & RN decided to postpone action on these controls.

All in all, there was little room for any doubt—taking the President's words as he moved from one subject to the next—that he was governed mainly, if not entirely, by a political motive; that he had reached the decision that the kind of changes that we were discussing—on prices & wages, taxes, etc.—were essential for the campaign of 1972. If there was any other motive, it either did not come to the surface or I was too occupied with my own thoughts to recognize it.

I assured the President that I would support his new program fully. I could do this readily, except for the gold suspension; and, though the President seemed unaware of this, I could not responsibly question what he did on gold—publicly. Moreover, I was aware of the margins of doubt on this question, and I could not be sure that my position was right and his wrong. In any event, as the meeting drew to an end, the President was obviously relieved to find that I would support him. He wistfully commented that the chair in which I was sitting was the one occupied by Khrushchev during his Camp David sessions with Eisenhower during the mid-50s. That evening, Saturday, Safire came to see me and told me how pleased the President was with my entire attitude and that he had said that he did not think that one could find another half dozen men like me in the entire country—that, indeed, I was a rare jewel.

The next day, Sunday, the President presented everyone at the meeting with a Camp David jacket, but he singled me and Kennedy out—we were also to receive some Camp David glasses.

The weekend confirmed my growing feeling that the President needs to act in a way that satisfies his hunger for drama and novelty, that he lacks true self-assurance and that [he] therefore requires some dramatic act to convince himself that he is a strong leader, and that his prejudices or shall I say principles?—will not survive clear evidence that the political winds require a change.

One byproduct of the new harmony is, apparently, that I can have a free hand in choosing Sherrill's successor. Previously, Shultz had come to see me with the announcement that the Pres. wanted me to know that he had already selected Sherrill's successor. Shultz did not name him.

[Closing the gold window dominated the sessions at Camp David, and what seemed so obvious about the entire show-and-tell on the part of the president and his supporters, who were all the attendees except Burns, was their uncertainty about what they were doing. Burns shared this uncertainty, for to solve stagflation took, he knew, different medicine from the traditional prescription (which was Keynesian spending to make up for business stagnation). The Fed chairman just knew that inflation was such a hoary danger, its results almost always unpleasant, that any policy would be safer if more conservative. His antagonists were principally the president, with his emotional ideas of the importance of great public surprise and public sense of movement, and Connally, a confusing factor, for by this time Burns was convinced the secretary of the treasury had no fixed principles other than to stay in office. Dwight L. Chapin was deputy assistant to the president. William W. Sherrill was a member of the Federal Reserve Board.]

Sept. 10 Friday. Met with President and Connally to talk over U.S. position at Group of 10 meeting in London. The President started out by telling us that he would talk very frankly to us since we were both "friends" and "politicians," but that he did not want us to communicate any part of his thinking to our staffs or others in government. He proceeded to comment on the needs of domestic politics—to maintain import surcharges, to press foreigners for trade concessions, currency realignment, and defense-burden sharing. This was clearly the mood of the country as evidenced by sentiment of Congress, particularly the impression of his address to the Congress on the interesting monetary and trade problem. We therefore should not be in a hurry to achieve a settlement, that in fact some "demagoging" on the President's part this year and next was good politics, and that a settlement should be postponed until after the election.

When I asked whether this meant that import surcharges could not be dropped before the election, President indicated that this would be difficult to do—unless, of course, we got truly major concessions.

This communication confirmed my fears that considerations of domestic politics would delay and distract serious efforts to rebuild international monetary order. In preparation for meeting, I had prepared a memorandum listing, country by country, the restrictive measures that had developed since Aug. 15. I gave this to the President and to Connally and proceeded to explain the special danger of an unfolding dual exchange system: that, to the extent that it succeeded in its purpose, the rate on the commercial dollar would be at or close to the old parity and thereby frustrate U.S. efforts to improve trade balance. President said he recognized danger; but—unless we hold firm—even worse restrictions on foreign trade could be legislated by Congress and that, after election, a reform of a more liberal commercial policy will again become possible.

I then told President that, while I fully understood his position, I did have to warn him of the risk he was taking; that much of his life has been devoted to strengthening the international order, that he would like to—or at any rate I hoped he would—go down in history as the President who reconstructed international peace and strengthened international harmony, but that a postponement of serious efforts to rebuild international monetary order would probably lead to a wave of protectionism and restrictions of all kinds, and that he was taking a chance of ushering in an era of growing restrictionism, trade wars, currency wars, and the like. He took this warning well, indicated that he would ponder the point; but I do not think I influenced his basic position which seems to be that he will act in [?] fashion only when he can again afford it; that is, after the election.

On the personal side the President could not be more gracious. He invited me and Helen to attend next Monday's Cabinet meeting (wives included), but I explained that I had to be in London. Previous Thursday, he invited us to concert at Kennedy Center, including reception; on Sunday to church services; and on Friday to his meeting with labor leaders (also another meeting in following week, which I could not attend); on Saturday to his meeting with Cost of Living Council. Safire arrived on Thursday with a request from President that I go on TV with a view to helping him get tax bill out of Congress.

Sept. 20 President called and asked me to come over within an hour. Hastily rearranged my schedule and spent an hour and a quarter with him. President was in a thoughtful mood. He wanted my impressions of the London meetings. Apparently, he was concerned about what he read of Connally's handling of the meeting. I told the President that Connally had conveyed very well to the ministers of finance and the central bank governors his own toughness and the firmness of the U.S. position, but that he did not show enough understanding of the position of other countries, that there was a danger therefore that the position of other countries—which have pride as well as problems—will harden, that Britain is now reflecting the thinking of the Common Market countries, that other countries are apparently in a process of establishing a common front against U.S., that they have enough power to frustrate our economic objectives, and that they also prove less reliable as political partners if we do not show a certain willingness to recognize their problems—as in the case of gold price. I explained that latter was a political problem for other countries, although some of them—quite wrongly I felt—saw also some substantial economic advantage. I advised President to take steps to get negotiations seriously started. We talked again about the advantage of U.S. toughness for domestic politics; but I warned that this advantage may be much smaller a year from now. He readily admitted this, and acted as if the thought were a new one. I suggested that he address the IMF-World Bank meetings; but he rejected this on ground that he may not have anything constructive enough to say. Instead, he would give a reception—which I thought was a very good idea but I also suggested that he invite Schweitzer for fifteen minutes before reception and have a quiet talk with him. He agreed to do this. We then talked about setting up a group that would work with Connally on negotiating technique and I strongly urged State Department representation; for the way in which the negotiations were handled could have far-reaching implication for our political position in the world. He agreed to do this, indicated that certainly Nat Samuels and probably also Kissinger will need to play a part.

President asked me to suggest what he might say in Detroit on international problem, and also to give him by end of week my thoughts on Phase II of price-wage stabilization policy. I agreed to do both.

[Pierre-Paul Schweitzer was managing director of the International Monetary Fund. Nathaniel Samuels was deputy undersecretary of state for economic affairs.]

Sept. 22 Bill Rogers called for an urgent meeting. Met him for lunch. He sees international problem much as I do, is greatly worried about Connally's ineptness in dealing with foreigners, is eager for an early solution of international monetary problem, fears a collapse of President's foreign policy, and is resolved to take a very active part in the activation of policy on import surcharge, gold price, and so on. He had heard reports of Connally's outburst in London, and was greatly concerned about the effects on foreign opinion.

Oct. 7 Attended Cabinet meeting on Sept. 24th. There saw President together with Connally. Cabinet meeting was devoted entirely to the approaching IMF meeting. President emphasized the domestic political advantage of the import surcharge; but he also noted that we had the responsibility for leading out of the present monetary impasse. There was a good deal of comment on the advantage of our not hurrying a settlement. Packard led off with the argument that time was on our side, since foreign trade was vastly more important to foreign countries than to us and they therefore could not afford or resort to discriminatory or retaliatory measures. Connally echoed this fatuous argument and so too did Kennedy. President seemed a little uncertain whether they were right.

At the private meeting, we discussed negotiating technique. President indicated that he was going to rely on Connally and me on the negotiating problem and tactics. He emphasized the domestic political angle once again, which favors delaying tactics on our part. This time I spoke up and indicated crisply why I could not go along with the thesis that time is on our side: first, because reason does not always prevail in human affairs—that pride, emotion, even madness may govern human and mental conduct for extended periods—that countries may not therefore focus on their long-run interests but may instead focus on short-run advantage, economic or political or both—that in fact this was already happening, as evidenced by the growing list of restrictive measures abroad; second, that there were some signs of recession abroad, that in consequence—if this materializes—we would not get as good a readjustment of exchange rates next year as now, and that—alas—we would be blamed for any international recession. All this seemed new to the President. We discussed next our negotiating stance. I argued that we should yield on the price of gold; and this was or seemed to be accepted—although it was also agreed that we would not disclose this until we seemed to be making progress in the negotiations. Connally made a proposal that we offer to drop import surcharge and also our direct investment controls (as if this was a concession to others!) if any of other countries would permit a "free float." I argued against this, urging that there wasn't a chance in the world that any such proposal would be accepted; indeed, that we would only anger foreign countries by offering (or threatening) to end our direct investment controls. Connally agreed to drop the direct investment part, but urged that the rest be kept.

I inquired again of the President whether he would invite Schweitzer. He later did at meeting that Connally & I attended on or about Sept. 29. George Shultz told me that Connally was very angry and opposed to Schweitzer invitation; he never gave me a hint of this, although he had ample opportunity. In any event, Schweitzer was invited, and acted like the damned fool that he is. More accurately, he is a pathetic man, always on the defensive one way or another. However, the Schweitzer meeting helped to improve international sentiment and this was what I wanted.

[Deputy Secretary of Defense David Packard was the cofounder of the Hewlett-Packard Company.]

Oct. 7 Talked to President by phone. He accepted completely my revision of his paragraph on interest rates. Expressed gratification over my taking chairmanship of Committee on Interest and Dividends, hoped that this would not be embarrassing to Fed, that my hand in this was needed, for a Stans or a Romney would not command the authority or respect required for success. I kept quiet for the most part. How could I disagree?

Nov. 6 Bob Ellsworth came to see me today and brought the following message from a source (unidentified) that he described as absolutely reliable: (1) The White House staff has formulated a plan to blame the Fed if Phase II turns out to be a failure. The argument will be that Fed failed to permit a sufficiently rapid rate of growth of the money supply; and this, so the argument would go, was responsible for the failure of the economy to recover as expected. (2) The President himself was organizing a campaign against the Fed—by pointing out to his financial supporters in Wall Street that the money supply has failed to rise in past 2 or 3 months, by arguing that this was contributing to—if not causing—economic weaknesses, and that they should write me—or otherwise get in touch with me—and urge a more expansive monetary policy. This campaign was supposed to have gotten under way some three days ago.

Is this a true report? There was no question at all in Bob's mind, and I trust him. Just three days [ago] I got a stern letter from the President urging me to start expanding the money supply and predicting disaster if this didn't happen. But I still await evidence—the kind of mail or the phone calls that Ellsworth described have not yet come my way—now I must go back in time a few days.

Oct. 28 A Quadriad meeting which Peterson and Flanigan also attended. Peterson presented a very civilized report—outlining a reasonable plan for ending the international monetary crisis. A discussion followed in which I pointed out that no realignment of currency parities, such as we wanted, would take place unless we agreed to raise the price of gold by, say, 5% or so; that if we failed to do that, and still wanted the French franc to appreciate against the dollar, the price of gold in terms of French francs would have to go down; that this would be virtually impossible for the French government—in view of its encouragement of gold hoarding by the French populace over the years.

At one point Connally burst out: Why are we always talking about what *WE* should give up? Why don't we emphasize what *they* should give up? This was unfair, particularly to Peterson and me, and I pointed it out.

The meeting was inconclusive on the foreign side, despite the need for formulating a clear policy to guide Connally in his Far Eastern trip. What would Connally do? His free-wheeling is dangerous; he is taking no one with him. Are we going to build a new world in sheer bluff and bombast?

On domestic side, McCracken urged further tax reduction. I disagreed and so did Connally. The President questioned me closely about money supply, and Connally did too. I was prepared thoroughly for the former. As for the latter, I reminded him that Treasury criticized Fed two months earlier on ground that money supply was growing too fast and that I then told him that they may soon criticize me because m. supply was not growing fast enough; that they had better, therefore, make up their mind.

Towards end of meeting, President told me he would see me tomorrow (Friday) to go over what I wanted to cover in private.

[Peter G. Peterson was assistant to the president for international economic affairs.]

Oct. 29 My purpose of this meeting was (1) to review problem of Fed Board replacements (2) to inform Pres. about Zijlstra's secret mission (to which I had referred in a letter to RN), and (3) to comment further on money supply.

When I turned to (2), President stated before I finished my sentence—"Oh yes, you mean Zijlstra, Connally told me about that." This astonished me; for there could be only one reason why Connally would go to the President with this—namely, to complain about me. This was very revealing to me; it meant that Connally was not a fair player—that he was working behind my back, while I took him completely into my confidence even after I began to have doubts about his character.

Since the President already knew about Zijlstra, but knew it through

Connally's eyes, I no longer had any reason to withhold from him the disturbing conversation I had with C about Zijlstra a few days earlier, where I learned that Connally was refusing to see Zijlstra. When I intervened he condemned the whole arrangement; denied that he had ever agreed to having Zijlstra serve as an intermediary; that he thought this was simply an affair of the central bankers—something that didn't concern him. I pointed out that the international monetary problem involved government, not central bankers; that finance ministers were inevitably involved; that he had agreed to the arrangement when I first planned it; that I consulted him again when I had the details worked out; that he then expressed a reservation about finance ministers; that I explained that the enterprise would be pointless without them; that the Zijlstra arrangement could be most helpful to the U.S.; that, however, if he no longer wanted it, I would call it off; that he then replied that we might as well go ahead since the intervention could be helpful; that since he didn't remember these conversations (Bob Holland was my witness—though I didn't tell C. this), there was no use arguing about the past; that we must now make the best of a bad situation; that Zijlstra was a distinguished personality who must not be rebuffed; that if Connally refused to see him, every capital in the world would soon know this; that an international incident like this would hurt him (Connally), the President, & the U.S. government, for it would supply evidence that C. did not want a settlement—something the Europeans & Japanese already strongly suspected. Connally fumed, even spoke of presumptuousness of central bankers attempting to deal with matters in province of finance ministers. I pleaded for common sense and decency, pointed out that C. need not tell Z. anything of value if he so chose, that—if he wanted to be secret—he would rule out flatly what we did not [?] and thereby make sure that Z. did not present any such thing in his mediation proposal! C. agreed to think about this, but I discovered later—from Volcker—that he was holding firm. Of course, I told the President all this in much abbreviated form; but President was concerned about C's not seeing Z, took notes on the point. President also advised me to talk over political aspects of international monetary problem with Kissinger. When I left, he said on parting: "Maybe we will need to change our position. It may be having undesirable political effects."

[Jelle Zijlstra was head of the Netherlands Bank.]

Nov. 3 Zijlstra cabled asking for appointments with me, Volcker, and Samuels. This required immediate reply. Volcker consulted Connally (then in Far East somewhere) and he said no. I then took matter to Kissinger, who called Volcker advising meeting with Z. Volcker called C, who agreed. Thus this foolish and time-wasting episode finally ended.

Volcker's part in all this was not manly. But he is an indecisive man, full of flaws, and anxieties. His petulance in this instance is, however, understandable; for, instead of learning about Z's mission from Connally (as C & I agreed he would) he learned it from a European at a Paris meeting. He felt hurt; but he lacked the strength or wisdom to sort out issues and excited C's mad temper, instead of seeking to curb it.

In my talk with K he made this astonishing statement: "President wanted me to talk to you about international money problem. He wants me to divert you, so that C can roam freely as he wishes." This is very strange—quite Rooseveltian. What a dangerous game RN is playing! And why?

Kissinger shares my fear of the economic & political consequences of delaying resolution of the international problem. We agreed to talk again soon.

Nov. 4 Saw President at Gandhi dinner; he urged me to go to India, indicated that he had informed Mrs. Gandhi of this wish; and asked me to phone him tomorrow.

[Indira Gandhi was prime minister of India.]

Nov. 5 Steve Bull called & asked me to come over instead of phoning. Kissinger was there for a couple of minutes. President stated that he wanted Kissinger and me to meet, discuss international monetary problem, and advise him on it; that he didn't trust State Dept and that [he] had no use for Peter Peterson as well. Then Kissinger left.

We talked about President's letter expressing deep concern about money supply. He told me that only Rose Mary Woods knew about this letter; that he will not discuss it with Connally; that he wanted me to know of his deep concern. I told him that I felt sorry about his concern; that he had some real problems to worry about, that he did not really understand what Fed was doing, that we of course would not permit the money supply to decline next year. He seemed reassured. We then talked about ways of manipulating expenditures for the election; he thought that Cap Weinberger could do that for him and that he would go after this at once.

The President's preoccupation with the election frightens me. Is there anything that he would not do to further his reelection? I am losing faith in him, and my heart is sick and sad.

[The domestic portion of Phase I of the NEP ran out after ninety days, November 13, and the result was a hastily put together substitution, not a freeze but two substitutes, a citizens' Price Commission and a citizens' Pay Board to govern advances on prices and wages. The boards juggled their requirements, and the Nixon historian Melvin Small remarks that during its first two weeks the Price Commission received 400,000 inquiries about its rules. This was not much of a Phase II. It lasted, to the president's relief (and Small admits with a considerable success), until after the election. *The Presidency of Richard Nixon* (Lawrence: University Press of Kansas, 1999), 210–212. Stephen B. Bull was personal assistant to the president; Rose Mary Woods was the president's secretary; Caspar W. Weinberger was deputy director of the Office of Management and Budget.]

Nov. 26 Met with Connally for breakfast on Wednesday, Nov. 24. He seemed to be in a calm mood, apparently interested in reaching a settlement with the Europeans and Japanese. This was a most pleasant surprise for me, as was my brief meeting with him upon his return from Japan the preceding week.

Volcker kept on reporting that Connally was in a belligerent mood. And that was a cause for my surprise. Also a few days earlier Bob Anderson called and expressed deep concern upon finding Connally "an angry man." Bob repeated twice what John had said in his most truculent manner: "I did not take this apart to put it back at a cheap price." What arrogance! What a difference from the August Camp David meeting! When I finally assented to the import surcharge and the suspension of convertibility, I stated that by these acts we were destroying the international monetary system, and that we could justify our actions only if we move at once to rebuild the monetary system, that not a minute can be lost, that if we delay the rest of the world will react with retaliatory or protective devices, and that the political unity of the Western world will be severely tested. Connally agreed at the time, and suggested that Volcker go to Europe at once to explain and start the rebuilding process. But he—and others—forgot what we originally wanted, or perhaps they never really meant what they said. And so I came back to the contrast between Connally's talks with me and his talks with Volcker and Bob Anderson. I found the contrast puzzling and disturbing, but not entirely—since his comparative calm gave me some hope.

At 11:30 same day, Connally and I met with the President. We talked mostly about plans for the Rome meeting. President made it plain that he wanted progress at that meeting; and that he indeed wanted us to indicate as much to the press—which I did later in the day. The President also made it clear that he did not want a final statement at Rome—that he wanted to get some direct credit for this through his meeting with Pompidou (Dec. 13 at Azores), Connally naturally agreed, hearing what the President had expressed, can it be that Connally spoke to me in a conciliatory manner because he already knew that the President was moving toward a settlement (Kissinger saw him upon his return from Japan, and he angrily inquired of him whether he had been sent by me) and that I had the President's ear? If so, his belligerent, angry, vindictive manner—in speaking to Volcker and Anderson, who never saw the President—becomes clear. Or so it appears. Connally continued to take a somewhat ambiguous—if not downright hard—line on the price of gold; but I patiently explained that no settlement is possible without small (5 to 7%) increase in the price of gold, and that we would be giving up nothing of economic substance if we agreed to that. My exposition was very simple, and I think that the President understood it, but I doubt if Connally did. Somehow, poor and wretched Volcker—never knowing where he stood on any issue—had succeeded in instilling an irrational fear of gold in his tyrannical master, whom he tried constantly to please by catering to his hatred of foreigners (particularly the French) instead of his capacity (not inconsiderable) for straight reasoning. This point about gold was left dangling in the air.

President at this meeting again expressed his concern about the money supply. I reminded him that I was looking after that properly, that he need not worry about that, that an apparent drive by White House (according to Ellsworth, dictated by President himself) to get financiers to write me alarming letters on this subject would accomplish nothing but harm to the Administration, for in fact two of the men whom Flanigan had urged to write me, telephoned me instead to report on Flanigan's maneuvering; this too I told to the President, and that Ziegler (by his stupid comments about Fed action on margin requirements) thwarted my plan to reduce margin requirements that very day. The President tried to defend Ziegler, and Connally echoed the President's defense; but their case was weak—and I'm sure the President knew it.

We later met at a long luncheon meeting in RN's EOB office—joined this time by Shultz and Kissinger; President had explained at earlier meeting that this was the group on which he was relying, that he had no use for Pete Peterson (second time he told me this) nor for anyone from State Department (though Bill Rogers was decent and meant well). The one new point that emerged at meeting was that trade concessions—even small ones, especially in field of agriculture—were particularly important to him, and that this could speed a final settlement from his viewpoint.

The role of the President's summit meetings was also clarified; he wanted the credit for achieving a settlement. And in the course of that discussion, he decided to have a meeting also with Sato—this one in early January in San Clemente.

The line-up at discussion became clear early in the meeting. I stressed the importance of our domestic economy—particularly, capital investment and stock exchange values—for an easy removal of the uncertainties surrounding international trade and finance. Kissinger stressed the political danger of a delay in settling the issue. Shultz and Connally balked. As I had already suspected, they had reached some kind of understanding (which apparently included distraction of Pete Peterson, Nat Samuels, etc.) on the international problem—which included resistance to changing the gold price and objecting to any kind of convertibility. I had talked to Shultz before on these issues, and particularly explained the economics of these policies. Apparently, Shultz was still wedded to a floating exchange rate, although he now acknowledged the need for a realignment of parities; but he somehow thought that raising the gold price, even though there would be no convertibility of any sort for two years anyhow, would inevitably restore the old monetary system; and he also thought that our making a modest sum of reserve assets available for a functioning of IMF would again reintroduce convertibility and thereby restore the old monetary system. Shultz's performance was an astounding exercise on the part of a man who should know that he has not the slightest understanding of international economics or finance! What a pity that this quiet, persuasive, but woefully ignorant ideologist has such influence with the President.

Here we were—Kissinger, a brilliant political analyst, but admittedly ignorant of economics; Connally, a thoroughly confused politician, suppressing his desire to punish foreigners in view of the President's moving away from narrow domestic political considerations; Shultz, a no less confused amateur economist; I, the only one there with any knowledge of the subject, but even I not a real expert on some aspects of the intricate international problem! What a way to reach decisions! No one from the State Department there, no technical experts to aid us!

All the same, despite Connally and Shultz, I feel that we're going to bring this issue to an end by this coming January. I am leaving nothing to chance in working for this outcome—so necessary for our country's peace, prosperity, and progress.

[The difficulty of deciding what to do, notably at Camp David, then at meetings with the president, Connally, and so many other individuals—both within the administration and with the "foreigners" Connally so disliked—required a seer, and Burns did his best. In no sense was he willing to take the president's judgment if he disagreed with it. Later, in 1974, it became possible to see that the Fed's policy of increasing the money supply, and of course not for President Nixon's electoral benefit, was wrong, that the inflation Burns so disliked and fought against became rampant. Sanford Rose, a respected economic writer, published an article, "The Agony of the Federal Reserve" (*Fortune* 90 [July, 1974], 90–93, 180–190) alleging that Burns was doing Nixon's bidding. Burns favored the article with a public appraisal: "There is not one grain of truth in his report." Scholarship has supported Burns but not with the detail of the present diary. See John T. Woolley, *Monetary Politics: The Federal Reserve and Monetary Policy* (Cambridge: Cambridge University Press, 1984); Donald F. Kettl, *Leadership at the Fed* (New Haven, Conn.: Yale University Press, 1986).

Georges Pompidou was president of France; Ronald L. Ziegler was the president's press secretary; Eisaku Sato was prime minister of Japan.]

1969 1970 1971 **1972** 1973 1974

The presidential election, with the president's challenger Senator George McGovern of South Dakota, was hardly a contest, and in no sense required the elaborate precautions involving Nixon-authorized break-ins of Democratic national headquarters in the fashionable Watergate apartment complex. But the tremendous chances that the burglars undertook were symptomatic of the exaggerations occurring throughout the White House's activities in every direction. It was the same sort of sick approach to ordinary problems of federal administration. It only made sense in sort of a feverish way.

The chairman of the Federal Reserve had seen by this time the single-minded concern of the president for his own reelection but neither Burns nor anyone else grasped the extent of the sickness. He of course noticed the sycophants, as he described them, who daily celebrated their own importance by their closeness to the President's House, as the capital's central edifice once was known before it became the Executive Mansion and then, during the supposed reign (it was nothing like that of President Nixon) of Theodore Roosevelt, the White House. The leading figures appeared to be the imported individuals from California, Haldeman and Ehrlichman. Neither appeared interesting enough personally to be capable of major mischief, until they proved otherwise. Suffice to say that as the scenario of mischief turned toward illegality it all seemed unbelievable, until it happened, with the full details not available until discovery of the taping system in the Oval Office and elsewhere near the administration's end.

Jan. 19 President telephoned yesterday morning indicating he wanted to see me and Connally later in the morning.

Upon my arrival, President said at once that he had learned of my deep concern about the budget deficit for fiscal 1972; that he had also heard of my drastic suggestion for dealing with the danger to financial markets that would probably follow the announcement of this extraordinary deficit; that he liked the idea, was inclined to adopt it, and that he wanted to discuss implementing procedures.

President had learned of my proposal from Connally the day before. Connally appeared to lean toward my proposal, but was not fully convinced. My proposal was announced at the very beginning of budget message, that the budget had reached a state requiring drastic measures; that unless such a step was taken the budget would be totally out of control; that the only way to prevent this is to legislate a ceiling on budgetary expenditures—a ceiling that would be absolutely firm, a ceiling that would apply equally to the Congress and the Executive, a ceiling that would permit no escape hatches whatever.

President indicated that he would do just this; that he would not leave it to Shultz or anyone else to write this part of the message; that he would do it himself in a manner that was absolutely clear, forceful, unambiguous; and that he would send me the paragraph or two for any editing I might wish to do.

President asked Connally and me to "leak" information on this to papers, for publication on Sunday. I later told Connally he or Volcker should do this, and that I prefer not to participate.

With this out of way, I turned to Pay Board & Price Commission, indicating that I had spent a good deal of time recently with Grayson, Judge Boldt, individual members of the Pay Board (public and business), and the entire Price Commission.

I explained proposal I had put up to Grayson and his Commission, namely, pick some number below 2½%—say, 2%; inform business firms that they may, if their business judgment so indicates, raise prices up to that figure; that they could do so without prenotification, but that they would still need to report the price advance, that they would need to justify it on grounds of cost increase; and that they could run the risk of a rollback if the justification did not stand up under analysis. Connally supported proposal—though without enthusiasm. Perhaps he was depressed; he seemed to lack energy at this meeting. Was he disturbed by Nixon's apparent nod in Agnew's direction? Or was it some temporary indisposition? For a week or more, his old bounce seemed lacking; and he seemed to be avoiding publicity—which he previously sought so avidly and so conspicuously. President liked idea. Decision was to give Price Commission a bit of time and in the absence of action—to make discreet inquiries (presumably by Connally or me).

Next I turned to Judge Boldt & stated my conclusion: that he was a man of exemplary character; that he was a true patriot—eager to serve his country as requested; that, however, he was still a judge rather than a political leader—that he did not know how to use a staff, that he felt his office required him (along with the other 14 members) to act judiciously; that he did not seek to lead the Board, that he would not do so as a matter of principle (he so told me), and that he probably would not succeed in a leadership role even if he attempted it. I then pointed out that time for a change was short; that the way Pay Board was going it was by no means clear that wage performance would improve; that if a change was to be made, this should be done within the next few weeks; and that my candidate for the post was Arthur Goldberg—who, I know, wanted to talk to President about Pay Board, and who, I felt, would be only too happy to accept the chairmanship. President was most interested in the idea; so was Connally (though he indicated he wanted to know more about his administrative skills). Decision was that Connally would inquire discreetly about his administrative abilities; & that President would have a meeting with Goldberg—at the least to get his advice about the way that incomes policy was going.

Upon leaving President's office saw Shultz in the waiting room—awaiting his turn to move in. I told him about the proposal on the ceiling (he had my thoughts a day earlier and was skeptical, without being opposed), and the President's intention. He shrugged his shoulder—this could not be done, since message was already printed up (what nonsense!). Later in day, I learned from Connally that my proposal would not get into Budget document (since the printing was already done), but that President would accomplish the purpose by putting out a statement before Budget Message went up, that this statement would proceed along previously agreed lines, and that it might be made on TV.

(Apparently, President did not realize that the Budget message could still be corrected—at a cost, to be sure, of money—by printer. How easily the technicians have their way at times even with Presidents!)

Later in day I told Shultz that Proxmire had indicated to me that Boldt might not be confirmed (hearing scheduled for Jan. 27), and that I wanted him to pass on this message to President. Shultz said that he would try to do this, but that he wanted me to know that he now rarely sees the President; that his influence had been drastically reduced; that this was a result of Connally's dominating personality and doing; that, I therefore might want to consider other ways of getting messages, if time was a factor, to the President. He sounded very pathetic and I felt sorry for him. He sounded bitter against Connally, & was critical of the President. Poor Shultz! He tried so hard to be a politician; he was entirely willing to politicize, if need be, the Budget Bureau; he actually did so in large part; and now he found himself the author of the most distressing budget in peacetime history—no longer a politician with influence, merely a technician but one who had earned the scorn of professional men—in short, having neither technical excellence nor political power to show for all his tireless efforts.

That Shultz was in this mood has been clear to me for several weeks, and he seems to have appraised his position accurately. Connally told me after the Azores meeting that President had no use for his monetary advice, and that he (President) could not accept Shultz's "doctrinaire thinking" or his "economic theology." Shultz told me several weeks ago that he now rarely sees the President, that he no longer has relaxed conversations with him as he used to, that his influence is diminishing, and that all this was Connally's unprincipled doing. Shultz had come to see me, also, to defend his handling of military budget which the President had criticized (apparently, as a result of my conversation with President).

Last Saturday, Peter Peterson cried again on my shoulder about his diminished influence with President: he too blamed Connally—correctly so; but I suspect that Shultz had something to do with this as well. Shultz could not forgive Peterson for his opposition to a floating exchange rate. Connally was concerned with power, not with Peterson's ideas; he had to get Pete out of his way, just as he sought to get practically everyone else out of his way.

Vanity! What vanity! Why do grown men act so foolishly?

[C. Jackson Grayson was chairman of the Price Commission. George H. Boldt was chairman of the Pay Board. Arthur Goldberg was a New York political leader. William Proxmire was a Democratic senator from Wisconsin.]

Jan. 30 Had Quadriad meeting on Wednesday, Jan. 26th, Shultz started out by buttering up President, telling him how wonderful he was the night before on TV; John Connally followed in similar vein. I felt disgusted with the two of them, remained silent; though I did indeed think that the President did exceptionally well, and I might have written him a note if the disgraceful manner of these two had not killed the desire.

Stein gave a gloomy report on economy. I felt he exaggerated the shortcomings and failed to note the significant improvements—as in the length of the workweek and capital spending plans; and I commented accordingly. Connally spoke in a similar vein, and was better prepared than usual—probably the result of Fiedler's briefing.

George spoke about the budget, how hard he was working to get cabinet officers to spend more energetically; this kind of talk by a budget director sounded very strange to my ears. Indeed, he complained that some government officials did not understand that it was their duty to spend more or else that they lacked the good sense to know how to bring this about. (According to reports of recent Cabinet meeting, George pleaded with all of them to spend more.) The President was pleased, urged that the spending be speeded up by April to May; that what happened later would not count so much. I could understand the President, but I found it hard to accept such unashamed politicizing of the Budget Bureau by its director.

Connally complained about the trade conversations with other countries; he spoke bitterly and urged punitive measures. He indicated that he would not make one cent available out of our international reserves to enable the IMF to function! I protested, pointing out that such action would undermine confidence in the Smithsonian agreement—particularly now, when uneasiness about this agreement was already disturbing foreign exchange markets. I also urged that the gold bill be sent up promptly, that we stop casting doubt on our own intentions, that we claim reasonable success in our trade conversations, and that we remove doubt about legislation on the gold price. Connally then became very annoyed, indicated that he too was concerned about confidence, and that he would move as fast as possible on the gold price; his annoyance was obviously directed against me; but his bitterness was reserved for the "damned foreigners"—and he raved on and on.

I commented on monetary conditions, indicated that M was not behaving satisfactorily, but that reserves were now growing rapidly. As for M, I pointed out that its behavior, while disappointing of late, was not a magnitude that we could effectively control in the short run. Some talk followed about the inadequacies of Hayes and Brimmer; and the President indicated he would do what he could to rid me of Brimmer. (A couple of days later the President wrote me a long and anxious letter about the importance of getting the money supply up. My, how he has been taken in by the monetarist talk of Friedman and Shultz!). I joined in the criticism of some of the Fed practices, but indicated that it was important to focus on the essentials; namely, that the Fed has supplied reserves on so liberal a scale that the banks were hunting for customers—that it was not lack of liquidity that was holding back the economy—that there was too much loose talk about monetary and fiscal policy—that what we needed was confidence-building policy!

[The Smithsonian agreement was concluded in Washington in December 1971 by the Group of 10 (Belgium, Canada, France, Germany, Italy, Japan, the Netherlands, Sweden, the United Kingdom, and the United States). It undertook to peg the dollar to the currencies of the mostly highly industrialized countries at central rates, allowing fluctuations of 2.25 percent, and raised the price of gold from $35 to $38 per troy ounce. At this price the United States promised to redeem dollars for gold. In effect this devalued the dollar by 7.9 percent. Several months later traders and speculators had moved against the dollar and some European currencies and fifteen months after the Smithsonian agreement, the dollar was devalued by 10 percent to $42.22 per troy ounce of gold. In March 1973, the G-10 nations announced they would let their currencies float.

M1 is the narrowest measure of money—cash and checking accounts.

Herbert Stein replaced McCracken as chairman of the Council of Economic Advisers. Edward R. Fiedler was deputy assistant secretary of commerce for economic affairs. Alfred Hayes and Andrew J. Brimmer were, respectively, president of the New York Federal Reserve Bank and member of the Federal Reserve Board. Brimmer had angered Burns because of making public statements at variance with board decisions.]

Feb. 29 Saw President on 14th shortly before his departure for China. He expressed hope, but also uncertainty, about the Chinese trip. He talked also a little about the later trip to Russia. With respect to latter, he shared feeling that very considerable achievements will be announced; that this trip would be a definite and huge success.

Our conversation covered numerous subjects. I warned him that budget for fiscal 1972 was much less stimulative than raw figures suggested; that there was much over withholding not allowed for; that revenue sharing would, at best, not lead to any expenditures this fiscal year; that advance payments to contractors are not equivalent to purchases of hardware or labor; and that the like was true of advance payment, on account of welfare, to the states.

I stressed confidence factor most; and indicated that social policies—as in the case of busing—have their economic impact. President was much interested in my view that busing was having an adverse effect on the economy. He talked indignantly about the horrors of busing and indicated that he was on the verge of taking a strong public stand against it.

I reassured him on the money supply; but he continued to express anxiety about this magnitude—speaking as if he knew what it was all about.

I told him that I was looking after monetary policy and that he need not be concerned about the possibility that the Fed would starve the economy. I told him that he should concentrate instead on fiscal policy, and I suggested that he get weekly reports on progress with regard to expenditures; Ehrlichman got this assignment at once.

We talked about personnel problems at Fed. President knew that Rogers would not have Brimmer for U.N. We talked about an ambassadorship; President thought that Sweden—preferably Austria—would be possibilities. I expressed strong doubt about Brimmer accepting an African post.

Hayes' recalcitrance came up. I told the President that he could do nothing about this; and that if problem can be solved at all, I would have to do it. My paying more attention to Allan Holmes, and making him feel that he is a partner, may pay off.

Had dinner with Agnew and our wives. Ted is extremely unhappy; he is informed of nothing and is treated with contempt by White House crowd—that is, when they choose not to ignore him.

Ted felt confident that the President would ask him to serve again as the Vice-Presidential nominee; not because he really wants him but because he cannot afford to drop him. He showed no concern about Connally replacing him on the ticket; and while this seems hard to believe, I am inclined to take him at his word.

Ted sought my advice about dropping out on his own. Reasons for doing it: (1) he cannot accept being so useless for another 4 years; (2) he could make $500,000 a year and thus put his family on a sound financial footing; (3) that if he ran with President again and the election was lost, he (Agnew) would be blamed all around; (4) that as far as his chances in 1976 are concerned, he cares little for it, but that he would have a chance on his own through extensive exposure in print, TV, etc.

I advised him not to give up: (1) because he would have feeling of inadequacy in later life if he did, (2) that he should not dismiss too lightly the chance of becoming President—by moving before 1976 into oval office or being in a good spot for nomination in 1976. But I also warned him that he might get hurt, since I was far from sure that the President would have him.

We argued back and forth. Finally, I advised that he follow his instincts, that they deserve respect; that I thought he wanted to stay on ticket (otherwise, why did he tell John Mitchell that Ehrlichman's leaving was a condition of his continuing); but that when the President asks him to stay, he should lay down some definite conditions about having an active role in domestic matters (as the President himself suggested in 1968). That is how we left it—except that we would talk again before long.

Ted Agnew is an honest man. He has plenty of guts and good sense. His estimate of Ehrlichman—as an immoral upstart and intruder—came through with special clarity. Somehow, I couldn't understand why, he spared Haldeman his scorn and contempt.

I feel sorry for Ted Agnew. I think Dick Nixon has no use for him and that he will be dropped.

[For shrewdness Burns was difficult to beat, but now and then he could make egregious errors about people, and in the diary judgment of February 29, 1972, perhaps because he wrote on the odd day of a leap year, he estimated "Ted" Agnew and was utterly wrong. Agnew gave a slight indication of what would prove his Achilles heel, that if he quit government and went into the so-called private sector he could make $500,000 a year. The State of Maryland, from whence he came, was enjoying rapid growth and the necessary nexus between industry and government needed constant strengthening, given the expectations of political leaders in the state, their moment being now rather than later. This was what proved Agnew's downfall in 1973, which caused awkwardness for years thereafter over whether he should have been allowed (as he was) to make a plea bargain and stay out of jail, as to whether his bust should stand on a pedestal in Statuary Hall in the Capitol (de rigueur for retired vice presidents), etc. Burns was a tempting figure to solicit advice from, what with the old-fashioned part in the middle of his silvery hair—like Henry L. Stimson of some years before, and Elihu Root whose tutelage may have had something to do with Stimson's part. Nixon privately disliked what the president described as Burns's stodginess and inclination to lecture, but in private conversation and to an uncertain individual like Agnew who had come out of the hustle of a developing state, it was tempting to ask advice. The long history of vice presidential misfits, the impossibility of fitting vice presidents into anything other than mechanical uselessness, was part of Agnew's position, a necessary part, shared immediately before him by Harry S. Truman and Calvin Coolidge and perhaps the most pathetic of vice presidents in the twentieth century, President Wilson's vice president, Thomas R. Marshall. Nixon's condescension toward Agnew was of nothing compared to that of Wilson. If only Agnew had copied the honesty and patience of his predecessors of 1919–1921, 1921–1923, and 1945.

During the second (and last) large gap in the diary, from February 29 to mid-September 1972, the economy functioned well, what with the cheapening of the dollar after the Camp David accord and the Smithsonian agreement. For Burns the result, a lowering of unemployment along with business prosperity, was no cause for celebration, for inflation picked up. Of all economic phenomena he disliked inflation the most. During these months when Burns's diary lapsed, the president followed the time-honored procedures of campaigning. Travel was by plane, no longer the campaign train—Truman with his whistle-stops was virtually the last presidential campaigner of that sort. But whether by plane or train, campaigning was fatiguing, and for that reason Nixon may not have realized that the election of 1972 was a foregone conclusion. At last, seeing the way things were going, the man who, Burns was sure, would do anything to win the election, relaxed as much as he could and declared, privately to be sure, that Senator McGovern's chance of winning was nil.

Allan R. Holmes was manager of the Federal Reserve's open market account.]

Sept. 16 Spent two hours in meeting with President, Shultz, Stein, Connally, Ehrlichman and Ziegler there. This was second of recent meetings (previous one on [?]), lasting 2½ hours (with Shultz, Ehrlichman: Ziegler brought in after 1 hour or so).

Fundamental impression that came through: President seems determined to keep expenditures down. He discussed this at length and explained that he wanted each of us to understand this; that when he was elected he was a minority President and cities seemed to be falling apart, that now he expects to be elected by a large majority, that House and Senate may go Republican, and that even if they don't he'll have much more support there; that he will get rid of OEO, of community action programs, that he had no use for model cities, food stamps, etc.

He explained that he didn't want welfare reform to pass. I first heard him say this on [?]; Shultz indicated this earlier to me.

Most of time was spent in trying to figure out how he could deal with promise made in acceptance speech to reduce burden of property tax. He seemed attracted to a proposal to provide a tax credit, up to $500, for property tax of people over 65; the cost of this would be little more than 1 billion. How was this related to the broad promise he had made? Well, one could be vague about this—savings on other expenditures, primarily tax reform; something Shultz called a fiscal progressing dividend (what foolishness!).

President was opposed to saying anything about tax reform. He wanted it to be made clear that there would be no value added tax under any circumstances now (before he kept releasing hints about this). He would not ask for an increase of the minimum tax from its present 10% (on people with substantial income); although at preceding meeting when I urged this, supported by Shultz, he seemed to be in favor of doing this.

What then was Nixon for? How would he use the opportunity of another four years? Nothing positive. His only values: to get rid of a lot of expensive programs that we don't need.

Opposition to tax reform was seconded by Connally to Shultz's great discomfiture. President indicated that contributions by the affluent to the campaign were a consideration. A week ago he argued that he didn't care about fat cats; that they ought to kiss the ground on which he walks no matter what he proposes in tax field.

All in all, Nixon appears to be more self-confident; his prejudices are coming to the surface again; he is more willing to articulate them; but no convictions are coming through, new or old. Clearly, he wants power; clearly, he feels that he is saving the country from the madness of McGovern; but I don't think he has any positive ideas at all as to what to do with his power—at least in the domestic area. Ehrlichman and Connally—both entirely amoral men—both very close to him—are not helping him to reach any convictions.

Ehrlichman has ingratiated himself to the point where he can invite

Ziegler in without even asking the President; when he can tell Shultz, during the first of these meetings, that he won't even talk to Eddie Cohen, etc.

Shultz made a sorry picture. He asked President what he should put the staff on: should he have them work on tax reform, on what kind of reform? President seemed perplexed by his defensive queries. Connally was chuckling inwardly and winked to me. Shultz was clearly upset and unhappy, partly because Connally was there, partly because it was obvious that the President was paying very little attention to him. He was interested much more in what Connally and I had to say; at preceding meeting in what I had to say. Shultz is such a good boy!

[Edwin S. Cohen was undersecretary of the treasury.]

Oct. 14 Had another Quadriad meeting on Oct. 9. The purpose was to survey economic and financial scene, following a long agenda prepared by Cap Weinberger. But meeting, which lasted over an hour and a half, turned into a monologue by RN.

President requested group to say absolutely nothing about future plans of Administration—not until election is over in any event.

He spoke with great self-assurance but said nothing positive about his plans for the future by way of policy or progress, except that he intends to pursue a tight expenditure policy. He indicated flatly that he would veto the $24 billion water pollution bill that was on his desk.

He spoke with feeling about the inadequacy of Congress; indeed he spoke of Congress with contempt. No leaders—none. Not Mansfield, not Scott, nor Ford, not anyone in fact. Two or three good senators—all from the South.

He condemned much of the legislation of his own years as well as prior years. He praised family assistance plan as being a brilliant idea, but stated that "we should have taken another thirty days to think it through"!

(President turned against his family assistance plans months earlier. The first I knew of it was just after meeting that dealt [margin note:

"Date:"] with [Federal Reserve] appointment of [Jeffrey M.] Buecher; he indicated to me it was too costly and he didn't want it. Shultz had indicated as much a month or so before this.)

President indicated that planning for 1973 would start right after election. He asked me to postpone my trip to Japan for this reason; that is, not go until toward end of November.

I had a brief interchange with Herb Stein.

Latter indicated that controls should come off after election. Shultz merely states that wage bargaining negotiations would be less troublesome in 1973 than is currently believed. I stated that without a lower wage guideline next year (4 or 4½%), inflation cannot be brought under control. President indicated that controls are popular with general public, but he felt uneasy about continuing them for long.

Apart from a doubt here and there, President was remarkably self-assured. He clearly expects an overwhelming victory at the polls. But something happened to the President in recent weeks; he is much calmer than he used to be, looks relaxed, seems to have more confidence in himself. August 15, 1971 was a definitive and decisive turning point in the President's state of mind. Another came right after George Meany and other labor leaders walked off the Pay Board; I was quite astonished at the relaxed way in which he took this (as revealed in Cost of Living Council meeting called to deal with this). He was not merely pleased; he spoke as if he knew just what was the right thing to do and that he would do it quickly and quietly. A new Nixon is emerging—a man who feels that he finally has not only position in the world, but great power as well. But I see no indication as yet that, apart from foreign field, he has the slightest idea what he wants to use the power for; unless it be to nourish some old grudges and prejudices.

[So far as the diarist was concerned, and presumably the president, the election came and went on cat feet.]

Dec. 16 Attended President's dinner for Cabinet. I whispered to him that I plan to go to Europe in early January. He appeared pleased and asked me to see him before I go.

President seemed relaxed and was very gracious. He proposed a toast to Agnew, then had Rogers propose a toast to Mamie Eisenhower—my dinner partner. Finally, President announced in his inimitable mysterious way that he was appointing a new Cabinet officer; that the office would be that of Counsellor; "That Arthur Burns first held the post, then moved on to become Chairman of the Federal Reserve Board; that this is a very powerful post, from which Arthur speaks only to God and me—mostly to God, since his position is independent—as it should be."

After this lengthy introduction and reciting names of two other Counsellors, President announced that he is appointing Anne Armstrong as Counsellor, and asked that no one speak of it to the press, since the announcement is being delayed until Monday.

Lucy Winchester told me before dinner that President asked her around 6 p.m. whether Anne Armstrong was coming to dinner; Lucy replied that she had not been invited; whereupon RN instructed her to get Anne immediately.

Anne was there. I asked her whether it was true, as someone had whispered to me, that she did not know before 6 or so that she would be named Counsellor. She replied in the affirmative; but went on to say that she did have conversations about a possible job, but that tonight was the first time she knew what had been decided for her.

[Lucy Winchester was the president's social secretary.]

Dec. Met at Camp David with RN. Quadriad group. RN kept us waiting from 10 to 12. Met for an hour.

Talked about controls, also fiscal policy. RN was relaxed, only half-interested. Not really well informed. Sounded less belligerent than before, but very political still. What little hope I had that he would see things differently after the election (and they've been eroding rapidly) was shattered. Still scheming, still politicizing.

I argued strenuously for a tough anti-inflation objective—1½ to 2% for the year. Shultz and Stein considered that too low, wanted 3 or 3½. RN came out, fuzzily, about midway.

RN expressed interest in my trip to Japan. I informed him it was postponed because of election.

RN inquired about Jack Sheehan. When I told him I thought well of the man, he went [on] to say that he will leave Sheehan at Fed and not move him (Sheehan had been asked by Malek to move to Undersecretary of HUD or Commerce; Malek asked Sheehan not to tell me this; Sheehan told Malek he wanted to stay at Fed).

RN talked out loud about giving us smoking jackets, for example; answered his own musing by saying we already had that; concluded he would do something else.

I stopped to talk to Ehrlichman once again about Geof Moore—who merely said he conveyed my concern to RN. Then I talked to Haldeman, pointing out stupidity of firing Geof: first, he is an outstanding man in his field—highly skilled, objective; second, it would be difficult to get someone else half as good for the post; third, there would be an outcry from economists and statisticians about the firing—so that this would cause political embarrassment to the Administration. Haldeman seemed to agree with all this. "We don't need that kind of trouble," he stated.—But Geof was fired anyhow! Earlier I had protested to George Shultz, who blamed Colson. Yet I wonder. In summer of 1970, at meeting in Pacific White House, Shultz criticized Moore viciously and stupidly before President; I came to Geof's defense, explaining he was a man of exemplary integrity, and that Shultz's criticism (which dealt with proper procedure for rounding numbers) was technically in error besides! So I'm not really sure about Shultz's position on letting Geof go. But I accept what he said about Colson; namely, that he kept complaining incessantly that Geof was putting out embarrassing statistics day in and day out. Just like Colson! (When I see him, I continue to ignore him. I look right through him, as if he were made of cheesecloth.)

[Commissioner of labor statistics, Geoffrey H. Moore was Burns's former student.]

Arthur F. Burns. The pipe was characteristic and served as a delaying tactic (its emptying, filling, and relighting) and a point of emphasis. Courtesy Richard M. Nixon Library.

Burns being sworn in, February 4, 1970, with the president standing behind him. Courtesy Richard M. Nixon Library.

With the president at the rear of the Oval Office; listening is John D. Ehrlichman. Courtesy Richard M. Nixon Library.

Burns, Pierre-Paul Schweitzer, the president, John B. Connally. Courtesy Richard M. Nixon Library.

Left to right, Burns, the president, Connally, and Paul W. McCracken. Courtesy Richard M. Nixon Library.

Left to right, Connally, the president, George P. Shultz, Burns (facing group), Herbert Stein. Courtesy Richard M. Nixon Library.

Federal Reserve Chairman Burns shaking hands with the president. To Nixon's right is Vice President Spiro T. Agnew. Courtesy Gerald R. Ford Library.

Meeting with the president, Burns in foreground. Courtesy Richard M. Nixon Library.

Cabinet. Daniel Patrick Moynihan is second from left along the wall; Burns is at the table at the far right. Courtesy Richard M. Nixon Library.

At Camp David during discussion of August 13–15, 1971. Front, left to right, Paul A. Volcker, Burns, Stein, McCracken, Connally, Shultz; back, Peter G. Peterson, Michael Bradfield (assistant general counsel, Department of the Treasury), Kenneth Dam, Arnold Weber, Erlichman, Caspar W. Weinberger, William L. Safire, H. R. Haldeman. Courtesy Richard M. Nixon Library.

Camp David, McCracken, Stein, Burns. Courtesy Richard M. Nixon Library.

Burns and Henry A. Kissinger. Courtesy Gerald R. Ford Library.

Diary entry, January 20, 1969. Courtesy Gerald R. Ford Library.

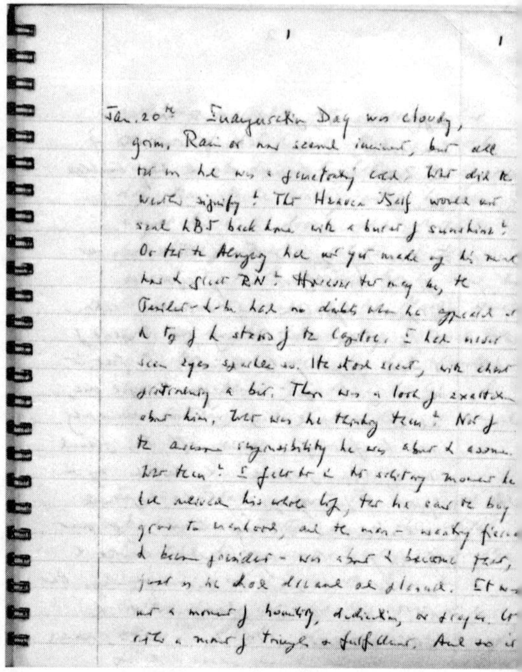

January 20 diary entry, second page. Courtesy Gerald R. Ford Library.

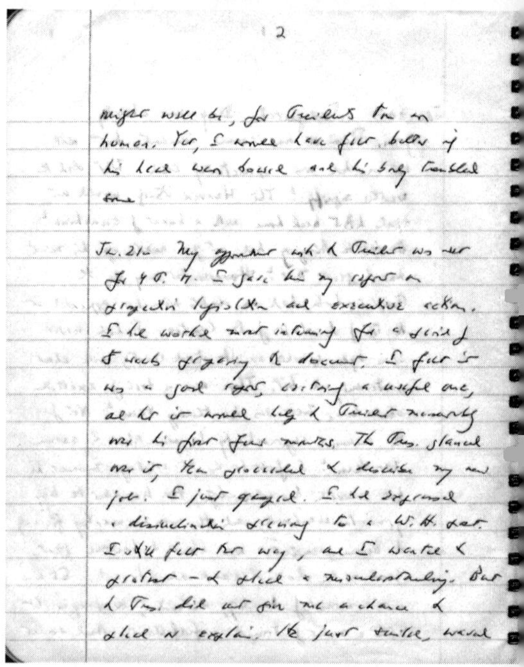

1969 1970 1971 1972 **1973** 1974

In 1969 at the inaugural Burns wrote carefully of personal triumph in the new president's behavior as Nixon walked down the red carpet, that trapping of presidential inaugurals that went back to the era of George Washington. Four years later he espied half boredom; it was the second time around. But in that four-year period beginning with personal triumph, and Burns's unease, the chairman of the Fed wrote of so many presidential errors he had become sure that a second term could only be worse than the first—which turned out to be the case. In 1969, Burns hoped for the best; in 1973 he sought to sweep back the waters.

The chairman's opinions of people were still, generally speaking, waspish. He wrote little more about the vice president until not rumor but indisputable fact arose; so coldly adverse that there could be no more advice to "Ted" along the line that vice presidents deserved sympathy by the nature of their office, whatever few had risen to higher office. Burns's opinion of "good boy" George Shultz changed. He had been too facile in judging this responsible member of the administration. John Connally's attraction as well as dangers diminished; his was a personality that could not rise for long above its real base of ordinariness. The other cabinet members seemed, as had been their cases earlier, shadowy and more a part of the scenery than anything else. He had written of Maurice Stans, whom he had known in the Eisenhower administration, that the department of commerce head had trouble finding things to do. All those important individuals around the polished cabinet table with its matched pads and ash trays and occasional coffee or tea cups blended into the table itself. No longer, however, did the position of the president, sitting between the flags at the side of the room, appear as important, whatever the scenery—officials' careful facial expressions of fascination with what the president said.

In January, 1973, a sign of the slump in presidential competence was the change from Phase II to Phase III in the plan to hold down inflation. Burns was not concerned as much with the domestic economy as with the international scene but had to watch both because of the interaction. He could see the weakening of III, despite the weakness of II, compared to the freeze of wages and prices that was I. Phase III abolished the Pay Board and the Price Commission, replacing them with a Cost of Living Council. In June there was a sixty-day price freeze. Upon initiation of III the stock market plunged and wholesale prices soared. It finally became necessary in July to announce Phase IV, continuing the price freeze until August, the phase nominally until April 1974.

Feb. 21 Attended Inaugural on Jan. 20. Watched RN's face & bearing intently, just as I had 4 years earlier. Once again, as he stood at the head of the stairs, he looked excellent; his head was high because he had triumphed; he was very pleased with himself—clearly. But this look, unlike the earlier event, did not last. As he moved down the steps, he relaxed, looked natural, indeed almost half-bored. Apparently, he was more self-assured, and was able—finally—to take himself for granted; to think of his new duties and responsibilities rather than exalt over his purely personal achievement and triumph.

The Heath dinner went smoothly. Toward end of evening, Bill Rogers ran up to me: "I've been looking for you all evening. The President was eager to have you talk to Heath." My answer: "I'm delighted. That's why I'm here tonight. Let's go." Bill Rogers: "Too bad, Heath left a few minutes ago." Not an unusual example of Washington planning!

Attended church services at White House on Jan 21. Passing through receiving line, President mentioned meeting my cousin, who had lived in Mexico, the night before. This I had heard from the cousin at the Inaugural Ball. The remarkable thing to me was the President's recollecting all this.

Politicians seem to have extraordinary memories even for—or perhaps especially for—personal detail.

Met with President secretly on February 6. George Shultz was there.

We laid out plans for devaluing dollar, getting Japanese to revalue an identical percentage, perhaps convincing Germans to revalue a little, and certainly convincing most others who count to stand still—that is, not change the par value of their currency. Another part of plan covered trade bill—to give President broad power to reduce or raise tariffs—the latter to be across the board, for individual countries or commodities. President had little to say except that if this plan suited us, he would go along. Decision was reached that Volcker would probably leave next day to start these explorations—Tokyo the first stop.

President referred to my recent correspondence. He promised to be tough in administering Phase III and asked me to quote him to this effect when I testified—as I was scheduled to do, promptly.

President also volunteered the suggestion that I could tell the Congress that if they want pre-notification, that is quite satisfactory.

President referred to my letter concerning Wilbur Mills. He wanted to know whether it would be sufficient to spend 1 hour 15 minutes with Wilbur. I indicated that it didn't much matter whether he spent 30 minutes, 1 hour, or 2 hours, that the important thing was the frequency of the Wilbur Mills visit. He called in Budd [?] and told him to make sure that Mills came by frequently.

[The White House meeting of February 6 marked an end to the Smithsonian agreement of December 1971—lasting fifteen months, no more. Whatever the finance ministers had decided, the central bankers were sure to try to protect their currencies. The meetings, such as Volcker was instructed to arrange—like the use of the words "float," "managed float," etc.—could not disguise the triumph of the monetarists in the United States and the end of the fight against inflation, save on momentary occasions. With the result that between the bygone year of 1936 and the present, the dollar inflated fourteen times. This was visible in the cost of a first-class stamp, three cents in 1936, forty-four cents in 2010. Edward Heath was prime minister of Great Britain. Wilbur Mills was chairman of the House Ways and Means Committee.]

April 3 Had Quadriad meeting with President on [?] to discuss state of economy, our domestic problems and the new international monetary crisis. On domestic side, I urged action on inflation first, repeating earlier warning, and stressing need to stabilize food prices—perhaps through temporary freeze. I urged some attention to variable investment tax credit. Got support on this from Ash, attending his first Quadriad meeting. President liked the idea. Why hadn't Shultz bought this previously? Here, as elsewhere he's always late. I also called attention to the low state of profitability in American industry; cited chapter and verse; this had not previously been brought to President's attention; he asked Stein to organize materials on this subject for Cabinet presentation; he asked me if I could come, or if it would be embarrassing for me—in view of Fed's independence—to do so; I indicated that I could and he was visibly relieved.

Bulk of time was devoted to the new monetary crisis. Shultz laid out the facts & informed President of Brandt's letter—the latter telling U.S., in effect, that Europeans were going to meet on monetary crisis, that they would seek a European solution, and that the U.S. need not fear that U.S. interest would suffer. President, who has nothing but contempt for Brandt, was angry; he indicated that he felt that he probably should send letters to Brandt & Heath indicating that we wanted to be there for we were very much concerned; he expressed doubt about the Common Market from viewpoint of U.S. and therefore opposition to any solution that brought the Common Market countries closer together; he indicated we need to alert the Japanese so that they too could express an interest in participating in the European meeting; and he urged us to meet promptly with Kissinger to work out a plan. Kissinger, after reading the Brandt letter, spoke without any doubt: what we had to do adroitly is to throw a monkey wrench into the Common Market machinery, for European unity in economic area would definitely work against U.S. interests. Letters went off to Brandt, Heath, and Touché—from President.

Kissinger continued his wrath over the international monetary meeting. He sent Sonnenfeldt to Copenhagen to inform Shultz of an intelligence report (apparently we knew everything that goes on at German cabinet meetings) that Brandt was very critical of U.S., saying that we didn't know what we were doing. Poor Volcker came back to see me, quivering. I calmed him down; after all, what Brandt said about us we say about many other countries; and Brandt is not entirely wrong in criticizing us as he has; and that the whole thing is mischievous, nonsensical gossip; and that we should keep our eye on objective—restoration of some semblance of monetary order, which is certainly of interest and importance to U.S. Shultz, whom I saw two days later in Paris, was also not impressed by Kissinger's fears. All in all, we did a responsible job for the U.S. and the international economy in Paris. But I'm concerned about possible later effort by Nixon and Kissinger to corrupt the monetary system because of some scheme of theirs, not clearly thought through, of breaking up—or at least causing difficulties for Common Market.

[Willy Brandt was chancellor of West Germany. Helmut T. Sonnenfeldt was state department counselor.]

April 22 Had lunch with Shultz on April 16. He whispered to me that the Watergate case is going to blow wide open, that his own involvement in White House affairs would become vastly larger. He implied but did not say that he may have to give up Treasury post. Swore me to secrecy. I interpreted all this to mean that Haldeman is about to leave, but I kept my own counsel.

President's pronouncement which followed was no surprise. But I will never understand why he waited so long. The Watergate case was so clearly a disaster—morally and politically. Why not cut out the abscess and be done with it? Why didn't he clean house properly? And why did he tolerate an obvious cover-up? Now that he has spoken out, why didn't he go further? Why didn't he suspend all whose names are now surrounded by a heavy cloud? Does he not realize that his authority is in jeopardy? Does he not realize that we have a crisis of governmental legitimacy? Does he not realize that the wheels of government may stop grinding? Does he not realize that more and more Americans fear, though they still refuse to believe, that he himself may have been the architect of Watergate? Does he not see that the rats whom he had assembled under his tent are now running for cover, that each man is now for himself, and that—sooner or later—one of his "loyal" henchmen will point the finger of blame (whether or not he has truth on his side) directly at him?

Some of these questions were answered by Garment at a meeting in my office yesterday. (Curiously, Garment had informed Ziegler he was seeing me to seek my advice on Watergate. Apparently, Garment is now serving as the President's counsel, though this is not too clear.) I gathered from Garment the following:

1. Watergate is merely one chapter in a long series of immoral and illegal activities in political arena.
2. Mitchell is undoubtedly implicated and so too is Haldeman. However, Ehrlichman may, perhaps, be clean.
3. Haldeman refuses to leave, insists on fighting it out, and the President is paralyzed, since he thinks that Haldeman will point the finger directly at him.
4. Legitimacy of government is now in question. Also, what the consequences may be for the economy and for our international relations.
5. Plans must be laid for bringing men who are "clean" into government to replace the rascals—Laird, Packard, Congressman Anderson, Rumsfeld, Shultz; perhaps Mills as Sec'y of Treasury (some of these names I suggested, when asked).
6. President must move quickly, before one or another of his rascals points the finger at him. The essential thing now is to protect the presidency. If Haldeman, fired or suspended promptly, does point the finger at the President, most people will believe the President and even those who don't will hesitate to drag down the presidency. All this will be more difficult if the President waits.
7. It is important that I talk matters over with Shultz—promptly and frankly.

Last Wednesday, April 18, I spent about 3 hours with President.

First hour—Shultz also there.

Later, Stein and Ash came in, so that a Quadriad meeting took place.

My main purpose in wanting to see RN was to try to persuade him to appoint Holland to the Board and Mitchell as Vice-Chairman. But before I could say a word, the President greeted me with the news that he had approved my recommendations, that I would have my men, that he was pleased with the selections, and with the Board. At my request, he urged Ehrlichman—who was then taking notes—to speed up the FBI check.

President looked ten years older. His mood was belligerent and bitter as he turned, it was not clear why, to the meeting he had with Jackson, Javits, and Ribicoff. He was particularly angry with Jackson who—he felt—was completely demagogic on the issue of Soviet emigration tax on Jews. He pointed out that he had assurances from the Soviet government that they would not enforce the law; but, as he put it, Jackson and the others wanted the Soviet law formally nullified. They would not be satisfied until they tasted blood. But the Soviets would never do this; hence, everything he had done to build bridges of understanding, etc. with the Russians was in jeopardy. But he, the President, is not going to take this lying down. He would go before the country, denounce the Jews and the Jewish organizations who were corrupting the thinking of the Senate, and a wave of anti-Semitism such as this country had never seen would follow. I had often heard RN talk mildly, but I also had never detected any trace of anti-Semitism in his make-up. Was this a latent anti-Semitism coming to the surface? Has the Watergate disaster destroyed his judgment? Was he merely exaggerating in private, as he often did on all sorts of questions? Was all this said deliberately for my benefit, so that I might take some part on his side of the struggle? I do not know, but I also do not think that he will carry out his vicious threat. My sole response was that, if he so wished, I would talk the matter over with Javits whom I knew well; he seemed little interested in what I said. Grudgingly said I might do this; he seemed fatalistic about the whole business in the sense that he thought that no one could change the thinking of Jackson or the Jewish leaders. Worst of all, he seemed to enjoy his bitter thoughts of revenge. After all, he could—and he surely would—go to the country—so he kept saying—and tell them what Jews had done to upset all his plans for establishing peace, reducing armaments, promoting trade, etc. Somehow, I was more puzzled than frightened by what he said; I'm inclined to think that he will pour out his bitterness in public, but my guess is that he will remain the politician and excoriate Congress rather than the Jews.

We also talked about the economy and this continued with Stein and Ash. These two advised the President to stick with Phase III. I told him that this course was hopeless; that a partial return to Phase II (to use another name, etc.) was essential, that the country was in a bad state psychologically, that, while business executives were in a euphoric state about the economy, there has also been a sharp deterioration of consumer and investor confidence; that when such a divergence of sentiment occurs, it cannot last more than a few months; that I could not tell which blade of the scissors will move, but that businessmen are generally sluggish and late in responding to events; that it was highly important to take steps to improve national sentiment; that the country is looking to the President for leadership; that he should not misread his recent victory in the House on the Ec. Stabilization Act; that Phase III is regarded across the nation as a failure; that a new plan was desirable; and that he knew my thoughts from the memorandum I sent him two or three days ago (at Ehrlichman's request).

In the course of the discussion, Ash and Stein made a plea for staying with Phase III or removing all controls. Stein argued the case ably as he usually does. But I dealt harshly with him, as I felt I had to. I pointed out that a return to free markets was good rhetoric, that rhetoric must not be confused with substance, that removal of controls would mean a return to monopolistic tactics of trade unions and many corporations, that I would indeed welcome a policy that established (or reestablished?) free competitive markets, but that Herb's prescription would reestablish the power of monopolists together with that of genuine competitors. Shultz said little but took an in-between position. The President indicated that while he disliked controls and questioned their usefulness, he also felt that he had to take some definite action; that the time to act was after the Economic Stabilization Act was passed; that he wanted a new program drawn up; that Shultz should do coordinating; and that the Quadriad would reassemble early in the week for some decisions.

During first part of meeting, President mentioned Watergate problem once. But he seemed to be talking to himself. Neither Shultz nor I took up the subject.

In discussing his victory in the House on the Economic Stabilization Act, the President stated that all this was accomplished by pressure from lobbyists and by contributors to Congressional elections. He mentioned cattlemen in particular.

Had a meeting with George Shultz at his W.H. office. I expressed my deep concern about the crisis in government that is shaping up; that the individuals involved in the Watergate mess were now conferring with their attorneys, etc. instead of attending to the business of government; that the President's credibility has already been badly damaged; that the ties of loyalty among the President's henchmen have been loosened or broken; that men facing a jail sentence besides disgrace will normally seek to protect themselves by pointing the finger at others; that such destructive behavior is already well under way; that even Haldeman (and who could be more slavishly loyal?) may point the finger at the President if he feels that he is being made a scapegoat or in order to lighten his punishment, that if events take that turn the President—and worse still the presidency—will be damaged to a point where orderly government, either at the domestic or international end, will become [im]possible; that the President must therefore act promptly, that is before any such finger is pointed at him; that if the President should then be accused by a Haldeman or an Ehrlichman or a Mitchell or a Colson, the public will be inclined to believe the President rather than his accuser; that even many or most of those who believe that the President is involved will keep decently quiet to save the presidency and preserve some semblance of confidence in government.

More specifically, I argued that the President should (1) suspend the high officials whose names figure prominently in the Watergate incident, (2) appoint an independent prosecutor in place of Petersen (however independent or innocent he may be, he is still a member of the Nixon establishment in the eyes of public); (3) some planning should get under way promptly to bring in men of unquestioned ability and *integrity*—perhaps Laird, Packard, Arnie Weber, Rumsfeld, Nelson

Rockefeller—perhaps move G. Shultz to White House as chief of staff and appoint Wilbur Mills (who probably wouldn't take it) Secretary of Treasury. Shultz added an important point—namely, the need to return to constitutional government, by giving secretaries the responsibilities they have under law, and by reducing the number and diminishing authority of W.H. staff. I reminded Shultz that when the idea of super secretaries first came up, I argued that the only right way to do this would be to appoint Kissinger as Secretary of State (since he would have the power over State and Defense) and Ehrlichman as Secy of Interior (since he would [have] power over national resources, etc.). Shultz's assessment otherwise was same as mine, and he indicated that Kissinger felt similarly. Kissinger joined us a little later; the above four points were gone over and we were in agreement. The next question was how to get these suggestions to the President, and we finally decided that Kissinger could do this best. He agreed to do so by next Wednesday unless the President calls him sooner. Shultz felt he was not close enough to do this. I did not volunteer, nor did either of them suggest that I do so; for clearly I am no longer as close to the President as the others are—particularly Henry. Henry sees things as I do; he understands Nixon—his love of the tawdry and devious, which goes side by side with some noble impulses; the President had already talked to him some; indicating that both Haldeman and Ehrlichman may have to go; the President, however, seems to believe that he can muddle through this one. I am not sure whether Henry will be direct enough or forceful enough; but I can only pray. May God save America!

[In the procession of events dealt with in Burns's diary there begin to appear, about this time, references to the Watergate break-ins, which had taken place a year before, in June and July 1972. The Watergate apartment complex contained offices and the Democratic national committee occupied a suite: Burns himself had an apartment in the complex and so did other high government officials. Upon the second break-in in July the police arrested several burglars connected with two supervisors across the street in a Howard Johnson motel. The supervisors were employees of the Republicans' Committee to Re-elect the President, the acronym of which was to have been

CREP but for which the Democrats quickly chose CREEP. Just why CREP arranged the break-ins has never been clear. Joan Hoff, *Nixon Reconsidered* (New York: Basic Books, 1994), has written correctly: "Of all theories to surface claiming to explain the reason for the Watergate break-ins, none has been adequately documented" (309). Presumably the burglars sought to "get something" on CREP's adversaries, the Democrats. At least one "bug" was placed in a telephone, but the question of why remained unclear. The arrests involved CREP, whose principal officers were former secretary of commerce Stans and former attorney general Mitchell. President Nixon learned of the break-ins a few days later, and consented to CREP's paying the legal expenses of the burglars and supervisors, a dangerous thing to do, which on their part could descend into blackmail, as Burns quickly saw. The president tried to cover up the break-ins as inconsequential "dirty tricks" employed by all politicians. In September 1973, discovery of a White House taping system entrapped him and the next year forced his resignation.

George W. Mitchell was a member of the Federal Reserve Board. John B. Anderson was a Republican congressman from Illinois. Donald B. Rumsfeld was counselor to the president. Henry M. Jackson was Democratic senator from Washington; Jacob Javits, Republican senator from New York; Abraham Ribicoff, Democratic senator from Connecticut. Henry E. Petersen was assistant attorney general, Criminal Division, Justice Department, in charge of his department's Watergate investigation. Arnold Weber was a member of the Pay Board.]

May 7 Attended Brandt dinner at W.H. President's toast was much inferior to his usual style. It was shorter than usual, and lacked grace. During dinner, he ignored Brandt (on his right) and the German Ambassador's wife (on his left) for minutes at a time, sitting with his chin resting on his hand, and just brooding. By the time we reached the entertainment hour he rebounded, and acted like his usual self.

May 2 we had a meeting of Quadriad. Shultz advised me not to quarrel with the revision of the Phase II program—on the ground that the President was too upset and could not concentrate. I didn't like this sort of advice; and yet, from a human point of view, it was right. I took it and did no quarreling with the emendations of Phase III; they didn't go far enough; but whatever they were, they were my improvements and both the President and Shultz had adopted them previously. But I could not keep honestly quiet when President asked if I had anything to add. Yes, I indicated—the variable investment tax credit; so that investment orders could be cut down. This was needed both to check the inflation and prevent a later recession. The President thought this was a good idea and suggested I talk it over with Wilbur Mills. George Shultz was very unhappy about this; he didn't want to do anything about the investment tax credit. In fact, he didn't want to do anything in the tax area at all.

Agnew called me and told me his new role in the Domestic Council (he mentioned this elevation to me at the Brandt dinner, and he attended Quadriad meeting—an extraordinary event) was being blocked by (of all creatures) Ken Cole. Agnew reported that Ken wanted Agnew to report to him (Ken Cole), that Agnew refused, feeling the reporting should be the other way around; that he objected because he had no confidence (and he is indeed right) in Cole's understanding or ability; that he objected also because he felt the VP's dignity left him no choice. Agnew went on to say that Cole promised to take this up with the President, but that Cole couldn't be trusted to do this, and he therefore sought my help.

I called President, but—as luck would have it—Ken Cole answered and put me through a series of questions similar to Haldeman's style. Poor Ken! He had learned what he knew (and it was mighty little) from Hald & Ehrlich; and he now acted like his teachers—undoubtedly thinking that this was the only right and proper way to act. Poor Ken Cole! He might have made an acceptable grocery clerk in [Fairtez?]; but here he was a wielder of power and the new keeper of the President's ear and door. Poor Nixon—too. Under circumstances, there was only one thing to do; I wrote a note to President about Agnew's problem (indicating incidentally that I was unable to get through to him) and sent it through Rose Mary Woods (my only reliable source for a long time now).

During my luncheon with Shultz last week, he indicated (as I did) that he (Shultz) would probably be asked to take the Haldeman post. We agreed that, unhappy though the assignment would be, he should do so for a stretch of 6 to 12 months, and then—probably—leave. Shultz would have to give up the Treasury post, which he loves dearly; he has some fine qualities—character and decency.

Shultz is very unhappy about the Evans pieces against him. I promised to try to straighten Evans out.

[The journalist Rowland Evans, Jr., was following up his book, with Robert Novak, *Nixon in the White House: The Frustration of Power* (New York: Random House, 1971).]

June 9 Met with President—a meeting of Quadriad attended also by Connally, Dunlop, Haig, and Ken Cole. Date [?]. Subject—the economy, what to do about inflation. Meeting was preceded by one among members of Quadriad plus Connally. President was upset, looked tired, clearly could not make up his mind. He seemed to be opposed to a price freeze, opposed to any fiscal measure, indicated that he wanted to do something that would be dramatic, I was sure that what he did would be harmful, but wanted to be effective for a time, and did not want to do serious damage. Stressed the importance of doing what is politically sound. Connally echoed all this, and—much to my surprise—opposed a freeze. Shultz & Stein wanted to do very little. I argued for stronger incomes policy, also for new fiscal measures—variable investment tax credit, and compulsory savings plan. As for a freeze, I would be for it—but only for 30 days, and on assumption that President needed time to make up his mind about the precise shape of new anti-inflation policy. Shultz & I differed about need to curb investment boom.

Several other meetings followed without President. We could not agree among ourselves. Shultz acted as chairman most of the time; Stein did on one occasion. Shultz made no effort to lead, no effort to convince others; he acted as if his whole mission was merely to assemble views, and put them (including, but not stressing, his own) before President. Shultz complained bitterly to me about President's negative comments about the inflation program and the energy program that Shultz had developed. Shultz has become increasingly unhappy. He resents, and rightly so, Connally's intervention. He resents also the need, most of the time, to communicate with the President through Haig.

Things are going like this for the most part. Shultz talks to various advisers, particularly me; then reports to Haig; who reports to the President—at one stage refusing to transmit a document because he (Haig) didn't consider it in satisfactory form (although it was a quite fair summary of the views he had collected & identified by naming individuals); then Haig reports the President's views back to Shultz. What a way to operate!

On Saturday, June 8, we held a long meeting. Haig had informed Shultz that the case for a price freeze & mandatory controls, in the President's view, had not been put fairly. Shultz was deeply hurt but proceeded to work out a paper (called Option II) to put this possibility (toward which President was now leaning) squarely before him. Connally had made one of his typical somersaults; this time (in sharp contrast to earlier occasions) he was in favor of an outright freeze of prices (not wages) for a period of indefinite duration. I insisted that it be limited to 30 days, and so the report went to the President. Connally also wanted interest rate freeze included in Option II; I insisted, and got good support, that this be limited to consumer installment loans. Connally also had some damned fool ideas about gold & they were knocked out.

I found this whole exercise disturbing & told Shultz that he was engaging in a technocratic exercise, instead of leading with a policy. He agreed, but felt he had no choice at this stage. He did say, however, that if President took Option II, he would resign.

Spent the day with Shultz & Stein at Camp David. Haig called indicating that President felt that Option I (Shultz & Stein) was too weak, while Option II went too far; that President wanted a freeze of indefinite duration, compulsory savings plan for corporations, & preparation for licensing export of foodstuffs. This was close to position I wrote to President on June 1 & June 8; but I took strong objection to a freeze lasting more than 4 or 5 weeks. Shultz communicated this to Haig.

Shultz is a very sad man. He is thoroughly disillusioned with the President—believes that he is up to his neck in Watergate affair, that he is devious, unprincipled. I don't understand why he puts up with it all, especially Connally's mischievous meddling.

Shultz told me that Dean had approached IRS and asked them to go easy on contributors to campaign. IRS director complained to Shultz, & he (Shultz) ordered that there was to be no favoritism. He told me that I was the only one to whom he had confided this. I appreciated this; but I couldn't help wondering why he had not confided this to the President. Was it because he believed that Dean was acting on the President's instructions and that he could not face the President on the issue directly? So it would seem; I can hardly recall a case when Shultz (in my presence) stood up against the President. I am sure, nevertheless, that Shultz is thoroughly honest and had avoided wrongdoing. He is, unfortunately, not a leader; and while he's become more pragmatic, he continues to worship classical principles of a free market (overlooking the fact that there is no free market to much of our contemporary economy).

[In 1973 the White House staff appeared to be in confusion. Shultz was seeking to unify its work. Major General Alexander Meigs Haig was taking the place of Haldeman, and Connally occupied an indeterminate position of White House power. John T. Dunlop was director, Cost of Living Council, John W. Dean III counsel to the president.]

June 14 General Haig called & advised me of the President's concern, reportedly conveyed to him by George Shultz, that I intend to attack publicly the President's new price freeze. I assured him that I had no such intention; that, however, I need to testify on June 26 and that I will be unable to praise the program; I will do my best not to cause the President any trouble; that I will try to help him; and that he can—and should—reassure the President.

At the same time, I noted that the new program was stupid from an economic and political viewpoint; that it would do nothing to contribute to confidence of business and financial people; that amateurs have gotten into the act; that Shultz, Stein, and I, however, are in large measure responsible because we failed to agree on a program and thus left the door open for amateurs and politicians. Haig agreed that this was the major cause of the trouble; he continued that the President was impatient with the doctrinaire (and non-objective) thinking of Shultz & Stein; that they had failed to analyze alternatives for the President with the promptness & objectivity that he expected of them. This criticism went too far & I said so.

I went on to argue that the 60 day freeze should be cut to 15 days; that we should hammer out a new program that makes sense during this period; and that this involved a new fiscal policy, emphasizing taxes or compulsory savings, besides a less restrictive and better balanced wage & price policy.

Haig reminded me of his phone call of two days [prior] when he conveyed to me the President's interest in my ideas, his constant rereading of my suggestions, and his desire to pursue my fiscal ideas a little later—once his immediate political problem was under better control.

The President's concern about my attacking him publicly apparently grew out of my telling Shultz at lunch today that I had to testify soon and that I could not defend the President's program very well. Shultz told me that he couldn't either, that he in fact was planning to inform the President today (at his 3 p.m. meeting) that he was resigning. He spoke bitterly about Connally & particularly so about Ash whom he doesn't trust at all. At most, Shultz mentioned, he would stay on through the Brezhnev meeting. Shultz also complained about Haig and Mel Laird shaping economic policy, and expressed view that decision to freeze was made four weeks ago and that he was performing function of the scapegoat.

July 14 Had meeting with President and others on July 10. An exceptional group attended—Shultz, Stein, Ash, Connally, Harlow, Laird, Timmons, Ziegler, Anne Armstrong. Subject—Phase IV; hence, the presence of the political people in addition to the economists.

President looked better than at Brezhnev dinner and previous meetings. He asked for advice that would serve the nation well, whether or not it was politically expedient. When the President talks that way, he has succeeded in throwing off some of his lack of self-confidence. And when he is really feeling well about himself, he has the habit of damning Congress, the liberals, the intellectuals, and sometimes also the blacks.

We talked about Phase IV. I argued for a bit of freedom for business enterprise—through term limit pricing, which would establish a zone of freedom. I got no support from anyone. Stein argued against it—this astounded me since he professes to believe in free enterprise. I've reluctantly come to the conclusion that Stein is a technocrat—that he'll try to do efficiently and well whatever the President may want, whether [it] makes any sense or not.

I argued for a tax increase. Shultz at one point seemed to support my position. No one else did. And Stein once again argued against a tax cut.

Ash boasted about his plan of trying to get expenditures for fiscal '74 down from 269 billion to 267.5 billion. I suggested that he get down to 260 or less. He said it was impossible. I pointed to the experience in fiscal 1973 when fiscal leadership provided results. I argued that Ash's program would impress no one in the business and financial community, that it was important to rebuild confidence, that our fiscal policy was not doing this, that monetary policy was carrying too great a burden. The President was interested. He went around the room, but I got almost no support.

The President has many shortcomings. He has few convictions, but now and then he gets into a euphoric mood where he wants to persuade himself that he's a statesman. But his sycophantic advisers cannot even recognize that. They know his prejudices and they cater to them. What a tragedy for this fine and noble nation!

[William E. Timmons was assistant to the president for legislative affairs.]

July 26 Had breakfast with Kissinger. He wanted to talk about himself and sought my opinion. First, should he accept the post of Secretary of State if it is offered to him? Second, should he resign within three or four weeks if the offer is not made? Third, will his Jewishness interfere with his effectiveness? Fourth, how should he organize the economic side of his shop if he does become Secretary of State?

It became entirely clear to me that Henry is most eager to become Secretary. I can't really blame him. He did say, however, that he was not at all sure that the President would have the guts to appoint him. He called Rogers gutless, and on an earlier occasion he called him a coward.

If not appointed, Henry felt his usefulness was gone, that operating from the W.H. he could accomplish nothing in the foreign policy area, that his appointment as Secretary would symbolize a return to constitutional government, that he and the President would therefore have some chance to make progress in the foreign policy area, but that it was quite uncertain—in view of the Watergate, etc. disaster—whether any progress was still possible.

We talked about Henry's loss of prestige on account of the wiretapping of his colleagues. He claimed innocence, that the "bug" on Halperin was placed by Hoover himself, that he had a letter to that effect, that the "bug" on others was also ordered by others, that he acquiesced because all this happened when he was in the W.H. only four months, was not yet trusted himself, and had no power to influence events.

We talked about Casey, Volcker, etc. Henry had no use for any of them in the economic area. I suggested David Rockefeller, explained why I thought he might take it and I agreed to think of other names.

We both agreed that our international monetary policy was stupid, that it could bring disaster, that other countries mistook our stupidity for rascality. We agreed to take counsel soon again.

Kissinger expressed the view that Nixon was anti-Semitic, that he had ample indications of this, but—being a very complex man—he also had occasional lapses into tolerance and idealism. I have myself no evidence of anti-Semitism; although on one occasion—when he was crossed by Jewish representatives on the Russia agreement—he shocked me by the violence of his reaction, by his prediction of a great anti-Semitic development in the country, and by his emphasis on his being willing to produce that if he cannot have his way on the Russian treaty.

I am reluctantly beginning to think that while Nixon is not at all anti-Semitic, he might well move in that direction if he saw a clear political advantage in doing so. More and more, I sadly feel that Nixon has all sorts of prejudices, both good and bad, but that he has no real convictions.

[The interference of ambition with conviction was nowhere more evident than in the conversation between Burns and Kissinger described above, wherein the latter was willing to place "bugs" on White House colleagues because he had been a presidential staff member only four months. Principle, therefore, required experience? In some sense that was true; one perhaps needed to experience sin. The explanation assuredly had awkwardness.

Then the discussion between the two men of anti-Semitism on the part of the president was altogether believable.

Morton H. Halperin was deputy assistant secretary of defense for policy planning and arms control, William J. Casey was chairman of the Securities and Exchange Commission. David Rockefeller was president of the Chase Manhattan Bank.]

Aug. 19 Saw Garment on Aug. 11; went over with him drafts of talk President planned to give. I found them belligerent, full of partisanship; and I thought they would prove disastrous. I then decided to write President a letter, advising that he assume a conciliatory tone, admit his mistakes, promise a new spirit, etc.

Garment talked about charges concerning Agnew. He had been informed by Richardson that they were very serious.

Couple of days later, Haig said the same about Agnew.

Had another meeting with Kissinger. He indicated that another two or three weeks will clarify his future—either the President names him Sec. of State or he is leaving. K. did not indicate whether he's had conversations with the President on this subject; but the only reasonable assumption is that he must have.

K. explained that the President was powerless; that the only way that he (K.) could have any constructive influence now was by moving to State. He sought my advice on this; and I agreed only that the time had come for him to become Sec. or leave.

K wanted names for the Economic Undersecretary. We discussed three—David Rockefeller, Gabriel Hauge, John Meyer, in that order.

K indicated he will have to lean heavily on me.

My only puzzle is: Why has he so seldom turned to me for assistance before this?

K's attitude toward Nixon is very plain. He considers him devious, guilty of what happened at Watergate, etc. He sees no future for him, since most Americans "regard him as a felon."

[In an entry filled with changes or imminent changes in the administration the comments about Vice President Agnew do not now appear shocking. The details, as they developed, were indeed that. The nation's second-highest executive officer resigned on October 10, 1973, the first vice president to do so. He pleaded *nolo contendere* to one charge of income tax evasion, for which he received three years of unsupervised probation and a $10,000 fine. He was forced to pay $150,000 in back taxes, which he raised by borrowing from his friend Frank Sinatra. In 1981 a civil court determined that he had solicited $147,000 in bribes from contractors when a county executive and governor of Maryland, $17,500 of which he received while vice president. (Small, *The Presidency of Richard Nixon*, 287.) Eliot Richardson was attorney general. John R. Meyer was an economist of transportation.]

Sept. 18 Had meeting with President. Harlow and Laird attended. R.N. looked good—much better than in recent weeks. He was in a constructive mood, showed eagerness to get on with business of government. I emphasized the high interest rates of recent weeks, explained that they reflected Federal Reserve policy, that this policy had to be continued until we got monetary aggregates under better control, that homebuilding was suffering already and that its difficulties would multiply.

Conversation turned to relief from fiscal policy. President asked my views. I presented again the case for variable investment tax credit or for refundable income tax surcharge. I argued that President's position that Congress would do nothing was unsatisfactory; that it was his duty to lead, and that he would be better off trying—even if he eventually failed. President asked many questions. Knowing that I would testify before

Patman's Committee next day, he requested that I indicate to the Committee that the President is seriously considering tax increases to fight inflation and lighten the burden on monetary policy.

President was favorably struck by the innovative character of my proposals. He referred to this explicitly in this manner several times. He talked about the importance of innovating—or at least appearing to innovate. And he urged Laird to go to work on my tax proposals, to put them in concrete shape. He emphasized the need for innovation—in general.

I inquired about the President's housing program. He talked about resorting to housing allowances. I expressed hope that if he goes this way at all, it should be done on a pilot basis. President seemed to agree. All in all, this part of conversation was most depressing. President indicated, or at least intimated, that he may be returning to Family Security Plan. He was unhappy about this—that much was clear; but he seemed to be returning to old plan because he knew not what else to do.

Saw Weinberger a couple of days later. In response to my question about his returning to family security plan, he denied this emphatically and, I'm sure, sincerely, what he was thinking of instead, he told me, was the negative income tax. He was amazed when I indicated that the two came to the same thing; that in fact, negative income tax went further in direction of guaranteed annual income. Poor Cap! An able man, but too busy to learn even the rudiment of his most important policy problem!

Testified next day. Decided to mention President's tax plan only on my way to hearing. Was not entirely sure even then whether to do so. Hearing lasted all day. In Shultz's absence, I called Simon to explain how I got into the tax act. My call was late, around 7 p.m.; or more accurately, I called right after hearing ended at 5, but did not get him until 7.

Shultz's outburst after Laird's statement, continuing what I told Congress about President's tax views, was not a characteristic performance. Usually, he stays—or appears to stay—calm, soft-spoken, dignified. His outburst was in poor taste, especially so in a foreign country, but it was understandable. He is probably angry with me, but he said nothing publicly.

Only after Shultz's outburst did it occur to me that President never mentioned Shultz though the subject was taxes! That was a characteristic Nixon performance—ignoring people's responsibilities and sensitivity.

Had breakfast with Kissinger on Sept. 17—yesterday. He wants my help in reducing Treasury's role in international economic area, so that State's role may be enhanced. Strange irony! The man who destroyed State's prestige is now being on the threshold of becoming Secretary, trying to rebuild State's prestige.

Kissinger confirmed that Agnew's resignation was imminent, and indicated that Connally would probably get the post.

[William E. Simon was deputy secretary of the treasury.]

Dec. 6 Met with President at Quadriad meeting. Others: Shultz, Ash, Stein, Dunlop. Meeting lasted nearly 2 hours. During the first hour, President was listless; looked sad, his mind elsewhere; shook his head now and then, but he was clearly not interested. Didn't say a word—as Shultz, Stein, Dunlop went through their paces. I finally woke him up by making two points: (1) contingency planning for ways of dealing with increased unemployment was essential, should get under way promptly—unemployment likely to be scattered rather than nationwide, but still sizeable, best way to deal with it—probably—was by planning a potentially large program of public service employment, supplemented by full listing of public works projects that could be speeded up in localities suffering from heavy unemployment, (2) A need for a crash energy program—a massive Project Independence—to be completed well before 1980—to be on a scale comparable to Manhattan Project and the space program, to be so designed and announced as to maximize the nation's sense of caring and desire for participation in an activity that will free us from dependence on Arab blackmailing sheiks.

President began taking notes and issuing instructions to Ash to plan a truly massive program for dealing with potential unemployment (not the minuscule $250 million program that Ash mentioned as a possibility).

President expressed concern about Simon. He indicated that he wanted to make major policy pronouncements himself. He indicated great interest in a massive program that he could announce for dealing with energy problems for the future; this program to emphasize reward, investment, and exploration—and combine magnitudes to be spent by gov't and by private firms.

Shultz & others urged a sharp increase in oil prices and reliance on market to equate demand & supply.

I agreed that it was desirable to have a free market carry much of the adjustment process, but that it probably could not carry it all, and that rationing therefore would probably be necessary later. Meanwhile, a tax plan should be worked out under which oil companies should be subject to an excess profit tax, while tax however would be forgiven if the amount of excess profit was invested in new facilities, exploration or research; in other words, if the abnormal profits were used for a national purpose. Shultz had a variant of such a plan—not entirely clear to me. President asked that work on this go forward rapidly, that the Quadriad meet again next week to discuss it, and that frequent meetings such as this be held in December. It will be interesting to see if the President will follow up on this plan; he rarely has in the past; and I doubt if he will this time. This will be a good test of his ability to govern again.

President informed us, pledging us to absolute secrecy, that there was a fair chance (according to Henry Kissinger a 60% chance) that Arabs will end boycott of oil shipments before end of month. President appeared hopeful, but indicated he realized that this may not at all happen. This possibility was a major reason for his going slowly on rationing. President indicated that even if this happens, Project Independence must go forward. And, of course, he's right on this.

President expressed some concern about low volume of homebuilding; but this subject was not pursued. He kept coming back to need to plan against unemployment and warning Ash not to be grudging about budgetary costs on all this; also on the importance of developing a massive Project Independence—one that would give the American people a goal and sense of purpose.

In meeting over recent weeks, H. Kissinger has referred to President as a "felon," as a confirmed "anti-Semitic" as well.

Kissinger tried to stop Shultz & me from going to [?] meeting of finance ministers on monetary reform. His reason: to show contempt for Europeans. He relented only when we assured him (Shultz and I separately) that no agreement would be reached, and that we could underline gravity of the political estrangement in our frank talks with the foreigners.

Shultz informed me that Connally tried to take over Fed and that appointments of Sheehan and Buecher (my *second* choices, not my first) were made in order to give Connally the control he was seeking.

Shultz informed me that President blew his top when IRS sought to audit his tax return.

Haig, who called me on Dec. 12 or 13, to tell me that Wallich's appointment at Fed is going through, confirmed my view that President has gotten back to work; he had done this for six weeks now, Haig stated.

[The entry above refers to the quadrupling of oil prices. The causes were partly the inflation of the dollar from the expenditures of the Johnson administration—the social legislation together with the cost of the Vietnam War. To this one had to add the closing of the gold window because of the rise of the economies of Western European nations and of Japan, requiring the inflations of the Camp David meeting and the Smithsonian conference and, a year and more later, the collapse of that agreement in another inflation of the U.S. currency. By this time the Arab nations, which received their oil payments in dollars, were supplying a large part of American oil. Furthermore American oil stocks were low. In the Middle East the Yom Kippur War, in which Israel obtained American arms by permission of America's NATO ally Portugal through the Azores, provided an ideal opportunity for the Organization of Oil Exporting Countries to raise the barrel price of oil. The pump prices skyrocketed. The era of cheap gasoline, which had lasted for decades, came to an end. Henry C. Wallich, professor of economics at Yale University, was senior consultant to the deputy secretary of the treasury.]

Dec. 16 Met on Dec. 14th with Quadriad. Gerry Ford attended meeting. Shultz had instructions (he so told me) to hurry meeting. This was obvious from President's behavior. He had no desire to examine Treasury's windfall in any detail. Gerry Ford—at President's request—discussed status of Energy bill. Everyone seemed to agree that House bill was unsatisfactory; but Ford thought that a decent bill might still be written in conference. President at one point indicated that he wanted to blast the Congress for its handling of the energy problem. (His pugilism had returned. He seemed like his old self, belligerent and defiant; except for a certain nervousness which was clearly visible.) Ford advised that it would be better to do this after Congress went home. It is curious that the President still doesn't realize that the only chance he has is to mollify the Congress. His Operation Candor is turning out to be a disaster. His income tax returns are not only stirring new controversy; their effect on President's reputation and public morals cannot be good; indeed, I would say, RN's tax returns are a veritable textbook in tax minimization via shady or dubious or slick transactions.

Had some discussion of economic policy. I took issue with Ash's pale proposal on public service employment. President supported my view and was stern with Ash (as he had been at prior meeting).

I argued in behalf of an energy program that went beyond Shultz's windfall tax. What was important is stimulation of entire energy area—production of coal, nuclear power, natural gas, exploration of all sorts; this could be aided by 5-year amortization such as we had during Korean War. This was desirable because of energy problem; it was desirable also for dealing—at least in contingency planning—an economic slowdown next year; and in fact, the rigid amortization should apply to a range of raw material industries whose supply product was in short supply. President strongly supported this proposal, Stein endorsed it; and Shultz acquiesced—though without enthusiasm.

At one point, President remarked: "Arthur has understood politics all his life." I didn't quite get the point beyond this being an attempt to compliment me.

President again made searching inquiry about Simon's doings. He seemed suspicious; concerned that Simon would make political decisions—as on rationing—and suggested that Shultz watch him closely.

President asked for another Quadriad meeting next week.

On December 15th, Mary Brooks told me about a private dinner she had attended a day or two earlier at President's house. One subject under discussion was Kissinger's role. Julie was reported to have expressed concern about Kissinger getting all the attention in the press; that President's role in Mid-East discussion was ignored. President shared this concern, by protesting that he talked to Kissinger every day; but that presses give him no credit at all.

About a week earlier at reception in Romanian Embassy, Mrs. Nixon told me that President was in good shape; 80% of the people, she whispered in my ear, are supporting the President. (Talk about self-delusion!)

On December 14th, just before meeting of Quadriad with President, I had breakfast with Senator Hughes of Iowa. Some two weeks earlier, at breakfast (prayer breakfast) in White House, Senator Hughes talked about his own conversion in a very moving address; he mentioned his new friendship with Colson whom he previously despised but now loved. I was deeply touched by this baring of his soul, and I too was moved to forgive Colson (who was present at this breakfast). I arranged to see Senator Hughes, and did so on December [14th?]. We talked about Colson, among other things. Hughes told me that Colson had told him that he (Colson) had wronged me, but that he did what he did on the President's instructions. I had thought so all along! What I still don't know is whether President simply told Colson to "get Burns" or to "cut Burns down to size," or if President outlined the precise course of action. It hardly matters; the two came to the same thing; but I may find out if Hughes gets Colson to come to see me and to ask my forgiveness (I have forgiven him in my heart already, anyhow); Hughes said he would ask Colson to do this; if Colson comes, I'll learn what happened precisely (or presumably); in any case, I'll be able to better judge whether Colson's reported conversion is real.

Shultz keeps talking reportedly about leaving. I'm hardly convinced—especially now, since after a long lapse—the president is seeing him again. Shultz is tired, but I think he likes being Secretary too much to give it up. I may be wrong. If he goes, I'll miss him.

Shultz has no use for the President, morally. He does not miss many opportunities to tell me this.

[Mary T. Brooks was director of the bureau of engraving and printing. Julie Nixon was the president's daughter. Harold B. Hughes was a Democratic senator from Iowa.]

1969 1970 1971 1972 1973 **1974**

At the beginning of the administration's final year—it of course would not last through the summer—Burns received a visitor who had repented his sins, Charles Colson, hitherto a White House operative imbued with the same "You've got your orders" philosophy as H. R. Haldeman. The question was whether Chuck Colson's conversion was complete. The Fed chairman decided it was.

The presidential conversation revealed by Chuck occurred aboard the *Sequoia*, the small presidential yacht that cruised around the Potomac, and the president had been drinking when he told Colson to leak damaging comments about Burns—twisted comments—to the press, concerning Burns's proposal to raise the salary of the chairman of the Federal Reserve, but not his own salary. Colson's press story said Burns wanted a higher salary. Repenting his sins Colson told Burns what he had done.

It was a saddening story with which to open the year, although for the history of the presidency it was a saddening year.

January 8 Chuck Colson came to the house to have cocktails with me. Senator Hughes doubtless got him to do this; he told me that he would advise Colson to come and see me, to tell me how and why he wronged me, and thus to cleanse himself by displaying remorse and hoping for forgiveness.

I had doubts about Colson's conversion, but they have been allayed. What he told me, how he said it; how he answered my searching questions—in all this he conveyed truth to me. I believe him and I'm now inclined to accept his conversion as genuine.

Here is what Colson told me:

Sometime in mid-1971, the President had Colson, Weinberger, Haldeman, and Kissinger with him on the *Sequoia*.

They were all drinking, engaged in lively conversation.

My name came up. Weinberger referred to a phone conversation with me; that I was "lobbying" for a pay increase for the Chairman of FR Board.

President was at once interested. He turned to Colson: "Get this out to the press. Let's teach Arthur something that he'll learn to be more cooperative."

Colson was upset by this assignment. He talked to Haldeman about it next day; Haldeman told him abruptly: "You've got your orders."

I questioned Colson: Did Weinberger mention my caveats: first, that I did not want the raise to go into effect until inflation was under control; second, that I wanted the raise to start with my successor, not with me. Colson was emphatic on the point: Weinberger did not mention it—perhaps he never got the chance, since President broke in with his comment about leaking my wanting an increase in pay to the press.

Apparently, President did not know—but didn't he remember our talk about this?—that I made those caveats.

I had guessed at the time that Colson had simply carried out the President's order; but I had thought of the President doing this in a mood of anger or annoyance—a momentary mood. Colson was emphatic: President was not angry; he was in a jovial mood. I did not think that Dick Nixon could stick a knife into anyone in a cold, calculating fashion. Colson was sure about his recollection; he also spoke with deep affection for the President. I think he told me the truth.

I asked Colson about two other "leaks" from the White House (through Shumway) that came about the same time—in fact, same day or day apart: (1) the proposal to "pack" the F Reserve—that is, increase no. of members and thereby reduce influence of AFB; (2) the proposal to put the Fed under the White House. Colson was quite sure these subjects did not come up during the *Sequoia* trip. His recollection was that Haldeman had mentioned these "leaks" the next morning—when he told Colson that he had his "orders." Colson went on to say that he associates these ideas with Shultz—that Shultz had talked about such handling of the Fed at staff meetings.

I told Colson about my conversation with Shultz; my reminding him of the conditions I laid down with regard to pay increase; his informing me that he remembered perfectly and that he had modeled his behavior—the salary of the OMB director—on my prescription; my advising Shultz sternly that I would not remain idle while my good name was being wrenched from me and my children. Colson then told me that Shultz went to see the President and told him all this; and that the President seemed unhappy about my having been treated unfairly.

Colson wanted to be sure that I did not resent Cap Weinberger's part; that Cap was nervous, unaccustomed to seeing and speaking to the President. I have no resentment; but I am puzzled. My recollection of the conversation with Weinberger is cloudy; but I'm morally certain that I must have informed him of my 2 caveats. How could I possibly do otherwise? Some day I may ask Cap. Or is it better not to know some things?

We talked a little about Watergate. I told Colson that I was sorry for him; since he was on the spot and that he would tell the truth about the cover-up, etc. He said that he would tell the truth, but that he knew nothing about Watergate, and that he had no reason to think the President was involved in the cover-up. At this point, a whiff of doubt passed through my mind. Is Chuck Colson's conversion complete? I accept the genuineness of his conversion; but the mind of both the converted and the unconverted can play curious tricks on men and we often end up believing what we like to believe—about others and also about ourselves.

Upon leaving Colson asked me to join him in prayer. He prayed simply and movingly; I thanked him, wished him well, and gave him 6 huge oranges out of a crate that had just arrived as I bade him good-bye.

On Friday, January 4, met with Shultz, Kissinger, Casey and Sonnenfeldt. We talked about Rome monetary meeting, about oil problem, etc. Kissinger had nothing to contribute about oil problem. In fact no one did—apart from the contribution I left in my memo on Abuses of Economic Power. Kissinger talked wildly—we should agree to nothing; we should not even talk to French. Not at all helpful.

March 17 Shultz told me on plane, returning from Rome on Jan. [?], that he had resigned twice, the last time having sent a handwritten letter to the President, that President did not answer or comment, but that Al Haig had indicated that Shultz can't do it now; that he (GS) is fully determined nevertheless to resign, for RN now is and will remain a president without power, that all RN is interested in is his personal problem, that he (GS) doesn't trust him, and—in fact—that he (GS) keeps wondering whether he is being set up for something awful.

We then talked about others who might take Treasury post—principally Wriston and Rockefeller.

Shultz indicated also that Internal Revenue Service had started investigation of Nixon's tax payments, that Nixon was upset over it, and that his offer [to the] Joint Revenue committee [to] decide what he owed, if anything, was his way of beating IRS to the punch.

During Rome meeting, Minister Hjalmar Schneider told Shultz and me that Nixon's prestige had sunk to so low a point that Brandt would risk his political future by coming to Washington; and that he, therefore, just would not do it.

Later, on January 30, Shultz told me that no one had talked to him about his resignation, not the President nor even Al Haig, that he is being totally ignored, that no effort is being made to get him to stay, that David Rockefeller is being approached for the Treasury post (after Walt Wriston had been sounded out with negative results).

What a way to treat a loyal and devoted servant! I can't help but think that GS would stay if he were properly (that is humanly) approached.

Some two weeks later, S. told me that President did speak to him, that he expressed hope that G.S. would stay another few months, and that he was developing doubts about D. Rockefeller.

S. also told me, by way of indicating how untrustworthy RN was, that Connally had told him a short while back that RN had asked Connally to take Treasury post again. GS did not explain when he heard this from Connally, but he did indicate that neither RN nor Haig had breathed one word about this to GS. Shultz, apparently, learned this sometime before his resignation; he was not surprised about RN's doing this.

David Rockefeller consulted me about taking Treasury post. I advised him to do so. About two weeks later, he informed me that he has decided not to take it then; that his main reason was that he felt that he would have little or no communication with RN: that RN had not seen him about this and that Haig could not arrange it. DR also indicated that he felt that WH had cooled off, that he sensed they were not really eager to have him take post. He was right in this judgment, but I did not have the heart to tell him so.

[Walter Wriston was chairman of the First National City Bank. Hjalmar Schneider was finance minister of West Germany.]

April 4 Saw Kissinger on March 8. He told me emphatically that he thought Nixon must resign; that he was no longer attending to business and that everyone knew this; that his influence was destroyed and that his (K's) effectiveness is beginning to suffer as a consequence. I quickly stated that N. will never resign, that this was not in keeping with his character, that he probably will remain as president until his term was up—since impeachment, I felt, would get nowhere.

Haig called on April 1, wanted me to know President's tentative plans with regard to Shultz replacement; wanted my reaction, since President (so said H.) wanted my advice more than anyone else's. The plan was: (1) appoint Simon despite, as H. put it, his grave shortcomings—a publicity hound, not reflective enough. Reason: job was virtually promised to him, and might prove embarrassing not to proceed with it. (My query—I didn't voice it—was it promised before or after Rockefeller turned it down?); (2) Not appoint Simon as Assistant to President; not give him a W.H. office; confine him to Treasury; (3) The broader responsibility to go in large part to Ash; (4) Make more use of Stein and when he leaves probably move Dunlop (whom Pres. likes, according to Haig) to CEA; (5) in meantime, use Dunlop more around WH; (6) draw much more frequently and more heavily on Quadriad so that I (whom the President admires more than he could say—so says Haig) could participate much more actively in basic decisions.

What a mess! Simon is clever but he shoots from the hip and may be (I don't really know) a political opportunist. Ash is surely a wheeler-dealer, not capable of sound principled behavior (also, so G.S. told me, he is heavily involved in gold stocks, and I therefore must make sure that he is never involved in int. monetary planning). Dunlop seems to have some of Shultz's qualities of working well with people, but Stein, who knows him better, scoffs at this description—he feels that Dunlop has an explosive, prima donna personality.

Yesterday, April 3rd, I ran into Chappie Rose, the President's tax lawyer and defender. I asked Chappie whether President had a case. "No," he whispered; later, came over, and asked me to keep this absolutely confidential. I'll do this, of course. But what a disgrace for the country to have its president make use of every tax loophole or dodge in the book! God help America!

Testified today. Raines, whom I considered a friend, informed committee that I was the best chairman the Fed ever had, then proceeded, in sly fashion, to intimate—perhaps he said this directly—that Fed (or was it I?) permitted the money supply to explode in order to get RN elected. I told him I bitterly resented this shot—how low can a man stoop to win a cheap one-day notice in the press! Is it worth while to burn out one's heart and injure his health in this sinful city?!!

[Irving I. Raines was executive director of the United States Tariff Commission.]

April 19 Kissinger called yesterday—a long day for him, devoted to holding the hands of the Latin American foreign ministers.

The afternoon meeting, which I was supposed to attend, as a member of the U.S. delegation (Henry has been drawing me into his activities, more and more. I've got more than enough of my own work to do. But, to the extent that I can, I must continue to try to be helpful, perhaps all the more so, since I'm not at all sure that Henry is a sound [he is surely very clever] thinker), was called off. I don't know why. Henry didn't stop to explain. And I was too busy to ask.

Henry's question: Jobert is trying to upset negotiations between

Israel & the Syrians. He is saying most awful things about Henry. Time has come to put him & France in their place. What can U.S. do, or the Fed alone, to cause economic trouble for the French? My reply: hard to see what we could do without starting difficulties that would spread and in the end, perhaps, engulf us too. Henry: "Would I give this more thought? It is urgent." I groaned that I would think it over (H. at times strikes me as a madman; a genius, yes; but he has a lust for power—a good pupil of Nixon's and Haldeman's, or perhaps one of their teachers? What outrageous thinking on his part!).

He had a second question: Would I talk to Ambassador Dinitz, and suggest to him that Israel must (should?) withdraw 5 to 8 miles on the Golan front? They really should do more; Henry, in their place, would. What he wants for me to do is to impress on Dinitz that if he (Henry) fails, U.S. will not mount another airlift and that Portugal, in any event, will not let us use the Azores. I promised H. that I would talk to Ambassador but I would not urge him. He wanted to make sure I convey to Ambassador his confidence. This is a very tough problem; I have admiration for what H. has achieved so far; but I'm troubled by his egomaniacal approach; I sometimes feel that if he can't succeed personally in a foreign policy issue, he would just as soon wish for the enterprise to fail or collapse.

On the French matter, I did tell Henry that I would speak to Wormser, that I would try to impress on him the need to improve U.S. French relations.

On the Israeli matter, I inquired why we were holding back the $2.2 billion for Israel that Congress had legislated. Henry became defensive; he is doing everything he can; that $1 billion has been made available; and that President refuses to allow more now. This may well be an accurate report; but I'm left wondering whether Henry has tried very hard (or tried at all) to raise the figure. I like Henry, but I'm not sure that he is fully trustworthy.

Yes, I recall now: Henry's big complaint is that Jobert is saying that the Egyptian disengagement didn't amount to anything!!

[Michel Jobert was foreign minister of France. Simcha Dinitz was Israeli ambassador to the United States. Olivier Wormser was a member of the board of the Bank of France.]

April 21 Gen. Haig called. The object of his call, he stated, was first of all why no meeting of the Quadriad had recently been held. The reason was concentration on the Watergate and impeachment problem. The recent subpoena had caused special, time-consuming problems. But, fortunately, the work on this is approaching completion. Next week, by Thursday, a complete report will be made; in view of probability of leaks, the report may be made public. It should change the atmosphere, and put various doubts to rest.

A second reason for his call, Al Haig explained, is the President's increasing concern over the economy. Bad statistics are being published on housing, interest rates; President is especially concerned about these developments. He is getting a lot of mail about little guys being hurt. President recognizes that some indicators of future activity are favorable.

President wanted Haig to tell me that he (RN) will soon start complete review of what could be done, by way of Federal action, to aid the economy—"to help psychologically at least." The President plans "after next Friday" (at another point, when I inquired about date, Haig said "next Friday") to have a meeting with his advisers "to take a look at whole picture; how to position ourselves psychologically." The following Monday, 27th (Monday is 29th); President will give a strong economic message before Chamber of Commerce.

I raised a question about my Russian trip, my [need] to know President's thinking on outstanding economic issues. I reminded Haig that I had written the President about this. Haig's reply: Let's do this on Friday, after the meeting with the several economic advisers.

I then raised question about Haig's call to me, explaining plan to appoint Simon and how others are to be fitted in, asking my counsel with regard to these plans, and suggesting that I either call or come over the next day to tell him what I think. I went on to say that I called more than once, that my calls were not answered, that two or three days later his assistant called and apologized and went on to say that he (Haig) would call me early next morning, that this call never came and that I naturally gave up. I went on to say that no harm was done as far as the Simon appointment is concerned, since I would have endorsed it; that as far as the other arrangements are concerned, I take it there is still time to get my counsel if they wanted it; that I was raising the point to indicate that our government may not function as well as it can or should if procedures such as I had recited are repeated.

Haig apologized profusely, emphasizing preoccupation with Watergate and the need, as he put it, "to spend a lot of time holding the President's hand." He also noted that he got the impression from me that I favored Simon's appointment. My reply was: Al, you read my mind correctly, but you did not hear me say this—since I withheld comment completely, in part because of your very request that I ponder the matter and communicate my thoughts the next day. Al then repeated his profuse apologies; I cut him short by saying that the only reason for going over the incident was to avoid repetition in the future.

Haig ended by saying that on the subpoena, etc., the W.H. will soon come out with something that they can, he is confident, stand on.

For reasons that were not clear to me, Haig spent a lot of time telling me about a "gut fight" between Ash and Simon; that this fight "brutalized both men"; and that president wanted "this to be cut out"; that President decided to give Simon less authority than Shultz had for two reasons: (1) George S. "couldn't cope with it all," (2) "President shouldn't delegate himself out." (Not quite what Ash had told me. According to Ash, President's chairmanship/Ex. C. was sheer façade.)

I now appreciate better what G.S. told me recently: Haldeman ran a much more orderly shop than Haig.

Bryce Harlow has confirmed this.

[William Simon was appointed secretary of the treasury.]

May 2 Attended meeting with President on April 24th. Lasted 2 hours 20 minutes. Those there: Simon, Ash, Gen. Haig, CEA man in agriculture.

At beginning of meeting, RN indicated he was concerned about housing and unemployment; that he wanted plans worked out; but that he wanted everyone to understand that the final decision would have to be his. Curious how his dogged inferiority complex comes through.

RN was like his old self through meeting. Full of sardonic humor—kept needling me about tight money good naturedly, but at no time suggested that I ease up. After my vigorous statement on the need for restrictive policy, he could hardly have acted otherwise.

This meeting demonstrated once again the advantage of preparation. I was the only one with definite plan for housing and unemployment. But whereas I sought to emphasize need for fiscal prudence which these problems were attached to, RN showed little respect for the budget.

All in all, the remedies he thought of or pushed were of the sort that liberals advanced, and which actually worked, ten or twenty years ago, but which are no longer working.

The plans I presented prevailed—or so it seemed. Ash was instructed to work out details with me and others along lines I had sketched.

May 27 Catherine Mallardi told me a few days ago that her sister Eleanor [per Joseph Burns' telecom with Ford Library staff on 1/18/2008, Eleanor Connors was a secretary then working in the White House] had informed her (upon my questioning this was confirmed by Eleanor) that one of the omissions in one of the transcripts had a derogatory comment about Jews; specifically, that Jews are leakers of information—Kissinger, Garment, Safire, and also I; that only Herb Stein was an exception. What an awful untruth! If only I could get my hands on this dastardly pronouncement!

Haig called on May 23 to inform me of appointment of Rush as coordinator. He explained that Shultz had two jobs—Secy of treas & coordinator—but that he couldn't handle these jobs; that Rush appointment was unusual but he hoped I would not disapprove; that the CEA chairmanship might go to Alan Greenspan or Rinfret; I indicated that I favored the Rush and Greenspan appointments, but that Rinfret would be a disaster. Haig told me of Quadriad meeting on May 24.

That meeting was attended by Simon, Ash, Stein, Dunlop, Rush & Haig.

President went around room, asking everyone what they thought of Rush appointment (with him there!), after explaining that Shultz's performance was unsatisfactory, that Rush's appointment was desirable precisely because he was not an economist, that he was to be a coordinator and not a policymaker. President was obviously embarrassed by appointment; though I don't know why (I consider Rush one of his better appointments). His unfairness to Shultz was offensive—needlessly offensive.

President was in good spirits, talked about the need to concentrate on economy, his aim to meet frequently with the economic group.

Most of discussion centered on inflation and need to bring budget under control. I took lead on this and was strongly supported by Bill Simon. Ash balked at idea of balancing budget or even reducing it.

I warned President that his national health insurance plan was inflationary and expressed hope that he will shelve his welfare plan. He seemed to agree. But can he stay put? And what, if anything, does he really believe?

Herb Stein's economic report was discussed, and President asked Herb to get a copy to me immediately.

It was decided that possibility of cutbacks in expenditure would be examined on basis of a document to be supplied by Ash; I argued that this was good politics as well as good economics, and informed President of change in Congressional and public sentiment that I have detected—namely, that people were now scared about inflation and would accept budget cuts as well as high interest rates. Simon supported all this. Ash objected.

[In the first paragraph of the above entry Burns referred to a sound-activated taping system. In February 1971, the Secret Service installed the system in the White House telephones including the telephone in the Lincoln Sitting Room on the second floor of the mansion, in the Oval Office and Cabinet Room in the West Wing, in the hideaway office in the Executive Office Building, and in Aspen Lodge at Camp David. Its existence was unknown outside the Secret Service and two White House staff members. In July 1973, the staffer Alexander P. Butterfield revealed it to staff members of a congressional committee, subsequently in public hearings. During the uproar that followed, the president refused to make the tapes available except for specific tapes and only after removing portions with personal references or points of national security. After the Supreme Court forced him to release all the tapes, the committee quickly discovered the "smoking gun" tape of June 23, 1972, six days after the second Watergate break-in, in which the president clearly sought to obstruct justice by a cover-up. A tape of June 20 revealed an eighteen-and-one-half-minute erasure that has never been deciphered, which the president's secretary, Rose Mary Woods, sought to explain as an unbelievable error on her part that occurred when she stepped on the wrong pedal of the recording machine. Except for erasures, of which there were more than one, the tapes are now available to the public at the Nixon Library in Yorba Linda, California, and in the National Archives and Records Administration in College Park, Maryland. Quality varies markedly, depending on external noises such as doors opening and shutting, helicopters landing or taking off, people talking at the same time, and nearness of speakers to microphones; telephone conversations are easiest to understand. NARA does not make transcriptions; archivists have compiled subject logs. Between February 1971 and July 1973 (taping stopped after Butterfield revealed the system), there were 950 tapes made, totaling 3,750 hours of taping. Very few individuals have had the patience to listen to more than a few of the tapes. Samuel R. Rushay, Jr., "Listening to Nixon: An Archivist's Reflections on His Work with the Nixon Tapes," *Prologue: Quarterly Journal of the National Archives* 39 (Fall 2007): 42–51. Catherine Mallardi was a secretary in the White House. Kenneth Rush was appointed counselor to the president. Alan Greenspan was a former student of Burns. Pierre A. Rinfret was an economist.]

June 24 Had meeting with President. Others: Ash, Simon, Stein, Rush, and Haig.

President began by expressing his skepticism about economics and economists. He wanted, so he said, to explore ways of dealing with inflation; but he felt, he added, that old ways do not seem to work, and that something radical—like dictatorship—might be answer. This, of course, he added is also no answer.

Stein gave a simple run-down on the economy.

I spoke next on interest rates and monetary development, pointing out that while interest rates were breaking records the economy was not being starved for money or credit; in fact, increases in money or credit were too rapid. I then turned to Franklin National case, noted its peculiarities, but also remarked that what happened in that bank was largely typical of what the larger banks have been doing—living off purchased money, letting capital position deteriorate, leveraging common stock, etc. I concluded by saying that basic reforms in banking are needed, that present however is hardly the time for carrying through more than a little in this direction. Markets are too nervous to absorb the necessary reforms.

Ash followed on budget. His comment was purely political—arguing that about only places where budget can be cut, politically, is in defense and social programs. This will not do; hence little to be accomplished that way.

President argued that military budget will go up by virtue of a coalition in Congress consisting of conservatives, liberals who distrust Russians because of their pro-Arab policy, or anti-Israel policy, or the President's pursuit of détente. These were interesting comments, especially in view of his trip to Russia tomorrow.

Simon made some comments about need to get better control over budget.

I told the President that his scoffing at the "old religion" of fiscal conservatism was not justified; that the "old religion" was precisely what people were yearning for; that I did not share Ash's skepticism about cutting budget; that Ash was wrong in urging that, defense aside, the budget could only be cut by reducing outcry for food stamps, veterans' hospitals, etc.; that sizable cuts could be made in the space program, for highways, for other public works, for agriculture, for revenue sharing; that criticism of expenditure cuts was unavoidable, that stakes were high, and that rhetoric against inflation is not enough.

President talked about his statement and asked each of us to indicate that another meeting on budget would be held, and that we should say that expenditure reductions are being thoroughly studied. I observed that this was fine; but that this, to be credible, would have to be followed by announced reductions. This was a disconcerting note, and President responded that our rhetoric should be muted.

As we were leaving, I urged President to re-establish Labor-Management Committee, to have this committee meet every two weeks or so, to preside at such meetings—and, in fact, to spend a full morning each time doing so. President said he liked idea; asked Rush to work on it—Will Nixon do this? I doubt it.

[In a series of economic remarks in the Quadriad in the presence of the president it was difficult to see any decisions, only the flash of ideas. The Fed chairman did say something thoughtful about the possible behavior of banks thirty-five years before the economic meltdown of 2008—wonderfully anticipatory but lost in the darker corners of the Nixon administration. Domiciled in New York City, the Franklin National Bank was the twentieth largest bank among the nation's 14,000 banks. When it failed on October 8, 1974, it was the largest bank failure in U.S. history up to that time. The Federal Deposit Insurance Corporation took it over and auctioned many of its assets to a consortium of European banks. See Joan Edelman Spero, *The Franklin National Bank: Challenge to the International Banking System* (New York: Columbia University Press, 1980).]

July 25 Had breakfast with Henry Kissinger.

He told me among other things:

1. President is doing absolutely nothing in the area of foreign policy
2. That he despises President and may leave in a month or two (he sought my opinion; I advised strongly against resignation)
3. That we have no government at present, that Schlesinger is causing unnecessary difficulties (even telling Israelis that he (Schlesinger) sought to help them during recent war, while Kissinger dragged his feet; that Simon is undercutting Kissinger (Simon is "well-meaning," but has a mania for publicity)
4. That early resignation would probably be inevitable for him if President is not impeached
5. That President gave Colson $5,000 to get Kissinger

6. That Haig was spying on Kissinger in National Security Council
7. That he, having lost 12 members of his family to Nazis, was certainly sympathetic to Israel; but that Israel must yield some territory on West Bank and that a policy of no-give would prove suicidal to Israel
8. That Makarios could not be trusted and that our sympathies were hardly with Turks.

I asked Kissinger whether he had any recollection of the trip on *Sequoia* in mid-1971 when President instructed Colson to go after me. Kissinger had no such recollection, and doubted whether he had been on *Sequoia*. I asked him to check his records to see if he had been along with President, Haldeman & Colson on such a trip. He promised to do so.

Had talk with Haig on July 22, wanting to check on Coldwell appointment. President had approved it, Connally tried to thwart it—wanting some woman in post; but according to Haig, President had said Burns must have the man he wants.

Haig went on to say that President considers Mills friendly and opposed to impeachment; that Mills is influential among Southerners; and that, in view of my old friendship with Mills, he hoped that I would urge him to work with Southerners. I told Haig that I could not appropriately raise the issue, that I do not discuss matters like that with Mills.

As it happened, I saw Mills today. He was eloquent about impeachment issue; indicated that he thought half of the Republicans would vote for impeachment; and that this would make it difficult for him not to do same. I listened and said nothing.

Mills indicated he hates Ash. One more plus for my old friend!

Going back to H.K. His experience was like mine: a failure to recognize the President from the transcripts. In my contacts, President has always been articulate, and rarely swore beyond saying "damn." In other words, he conducted himself with dignity. But, as the transcripts show, he spoke in a private jargon, sounded illiterate, and used foul language all over the place, in his conversation with H, E, & Colson. Kissinger said his experience was exactly same as mine, and that he could not recognize the man he thought he knew—as he read the transcripts.

Apparently, the President was not fully comfortable with either Kissinger or me. The transcripts clear up the old mystery why he spent so much time with vulgarians like Haldeman, etc.; he could relax with them and be himself.

[In this, the final entry of the diary, Burns again referred to the transcripts. The taping system entrapped the president, who resigned on August 9. James R. Schlesinger was secretary of defense. The archbishop was leader of the Cypriot Greeks. Philip E. Coldwell was appointed president of the Dallas Federal Reserve Bank.]

Index